Library of the Chathams
Chatham, New Jersey

Gift of

The Woman's Club of Chatham

2013

Praise for

MOGUL, MOM, & MAID
and Liz O'Donnell

"This is the perfect moment for this important book which advances the conversation about how to provide and care for yourself and your family, while living a happy and meaningful life. Could there be a more important topic? Liz O'Donnell does a wonderful job combining the stories of real women, with helpful research, and specific action steps. Well done."
—Jacki Zehner, CEO, Women Moving Millions and former partner and managing director, Goldman Sachs

"In *Mogul, Mom, & Maid*, women breadwinners share their honest views on the challenges they face in reaching their true potential. While many of those challenges manifest at the conference table, they also manifest at the kitchen table. In giving voice to these women and the issues they face managing both work and home, O'Donnell helps crack the code on what's holding women back and outlines practical steps to help women, their partners, and their employers redefine women's relationships with and access to power."
—Gloria Feldt, co-founder of Take The Lead and author, *No Excuses: 9 Ways Women Can Change How We Think About Power*

"O'Donnell gives us straight talk and a revealing inside look at an unsung and besieged heroine: the working woman. Drawing on scores of interviews, O'Donnell is a perceptive guide to the challenges posed by husbands (when present), children, workplaces, and women's own hopes and doubts. Racing to keep pace with a relentless daily calendar and to-do list, the women you will meet here are gutsy pioneers who just might lead us toward a fairer society and a more sustainable balance between work and family."
—Charles Derber, professor of sociology at Boston College, co-author, *The New Feminized Majority: How Democrats Can Change America with Women's Values and Sociopathic Society: A People's Sociology of the United States*

"If you think you've read it all about having it all, you haven't read *Mogul, Mom, & Maid*. Even as moguls debate about 'bringing home bacon and frying it up in the pan,' through a deft mix of research, interviews, and her Hello Ladies' unique voice, Liz O'Donnell provides a refreshingly candid look at the actual bacon-making of a working mom (and maid's) life.

—Whitney Johnson, cofounder, Rose Park Advisors,
author, *Dare, Dream, Do: Remarkable Things Happen
When You Dare to Dream*

"*Mogul, Mom, & Maid* should have been written twenty-five years ago! We would have saved ourselves a collective wandering in the desert. A must-read for anyone looking for a more balanced life, no matter your sex!"

—Larry Weber, chairman & CEO, W2 Group, Inc.

"*Mogul, Mom, & Maid* is unflinchingly honest about the challenges modern women face as they juggle professional and personal roles. O'Donnell shares her own stories—as well as those from the hundred women she interviewed, many of them breadwinners—and does not pretend there are easy answers. Yet, with humor, she offers useful and practical advice for women and their employers. Lean in to this book—and share it with the women whose happiness matters to you."

—Carol Frohlinger, co-founder, Negotiation Women, Inc.,
www.negotiatingwomen.com

"Liz tells her own and other women's stories with passion, humor, respect and curiosity. She is a woman on a mission, so here's to Liz—mom, mogul, maid, and missionary. Mission achieved. A book for every woman and man juggling home, marriage, family and career."

—Dr. Anne Perschel, leadership and business psychologist,
Germane Consulting, Co-founder, 3Plus International.
Women-Worth-Knowing

"With *Mogul, Mom, & Maid*, Liz O' Donnell strikes an inspiring balance between being comprehensive and compassionate. She tells stories of real women like you and me, as well as other women we might not know, and does this with warmth, insight, and empathy. Liz O'Donnell shares the many truths about what it really means to be a woman, a mom, a wife, and a manager. It also goes further to suggest ways that individually and together we can create new truths. *Mogul, Mom, & Maid* will help you see opportunities in the complexities of the big picture. Even better, it will inspire you to make meaningful changes right where you are."

—CV Harquail, PhD, consultant,
AuthenticOrganizations.com, management faculty,
Stevens Institute of Technology

"O'Donnell goes beyond the statistics and takes a hard, first-hand look at how women's responsibilities at home are impeding their career advancement…and how negotiation can change the game for women everywhere."

—Victoria Pynchon, author,
*The Grownups' ABC's of Conflict Resolution
and Success as a Mediator for Dummies*

MOGUL,
MOM,
& MAID

THE BALANCING ACT of the MODERN WOMAN

Liz O'Donnell

bibliomotion
books + media

First published by Bibliomotion, Inc.

33 Manchester Road
Brookline, MA 02446
Tel: 617-934-2427
www.bibliomotion.com

Printed in the United States of America

Library of Congress Cataloging-in-Publication Data

O'Donnell, Liz.
  Mogul, mom, & maid : the balancing act of the modern woman / Liz O'Donnell.
    pages cm
  Summary: "Mogul, Mom, & Maid takes an honest look at how women are balancing home life and career. Liz O'Donnell goes beyond statistics and tells the stories of women all across America who are juggling careers, motherhood, marriage, and households"— Provided by publisher.
  ISBN 978-1-937134-73-0 (hardback) — ISBN 978-1-937134-74-7 (ebook) — ISBN 978-1-937134-75-4 (enhanced ebook)
  1. Women employees. 2. Career development. 3. Motherhood.
I. Title. II. Title: Mogul, mom and maid.
  HD6053.O36 2013
  331.40973—dc23
                                                        2013028024

CONTENTS

ACKNOWLEDGMENTS

First and foremost thank you to all of the women who opened up your lives and shared your stories with me. Thank you to Jean, Kim, and Jessica, for opening your living rooms to me, and to Kyle at Whole Foods who filled your kitchens with dessert. Thank you to Nancy and Oz for sharing your home with me and giving me a beautiful writing retreat. Thank you to Nancy C. for your counsel, Chrysula for introducing me to Whitney, and Whitney for introducing me to Bibliomotion.

Many thanks to Jill, Erika, Shevaun, and all of the staff, authors, and friends of Bibliomotion who have created more than a company—they've created a dynamic community.

Thank you to my immediate and extended family members, my village in Dedham, my friends across the country, as well as across the blogosphere and Twittersphere, and at work. I am grateful for the support, encouragement, coaching, chocolate, champagne, and connections. I want to call you out by name but would hate to forget any of you. Never before have I asked so much of so many and I want to return all of the favors—that's how women work.

And finally, love and gratitude to Kevin, Joe, and Kate who always support me. You are the reason I love being a working mother.

INTRODUCTION

While the roles of women at work and at home have been discussed and debated since the days of Rosie the Riveter, in the past few years we've heard and read more declarations about women who work outside the home than ever before. Is it the end of men? Are women the richer sex? Can we have it all or not? Should we be leaning in or opting out? And is motherhood really the most important job?

The headlines, and the statistics behind them, don't tell the whole story. The truth is, more and more women today are breadwinners, and these breadwinners are struggling. They are caught in a perfect storm of male-dominated culture at work, traditional social norms at home, and outdated schedules in the school system.

Mogul, Mom, & Maid: The Balancing Act of the Modern Woman takes an honest look at how women are balancing home life and career. This book goes beyond the statistics and tells the stories of real women all across America who are juggling careers, motherhood, and marriage. Some of them are thriving, some of them are striving, and many of them are ducking, staying clear of the glass ceiling instead of trying to shatter it. They're working because they need the money, but they've got little motivation beyond their financial survival.

So much has changed since Lisa Belkin sent ripples through feminist circles with her 2003 *New York Times* article about women opting out of their careers. Today, women make up almost 60 percent of U.S. college students and earn the majority of postgraduate degrees,[1] including doctor's degrees.[2] Among married couples who both work, wives earn an average of 38 percent of family income,[3] and nearly 40 percent of the women are outearning their husbands. That's an increase of more than 50 percent in twenty years.[4] Some economists predict that, in just a few years, more families will be supported by women than by men.

Things have shifted at home too. In recent years, husbands have doubled their share of housework and tripled their share of child care,[5] while women's housework hours have dropped. But despite the many, and in some case dramatic, shifts, some things haven't changed at all.

Yes, men are doing more housework than they've ever done, but they were starting from a very low percentage. According to the *American Time Use Survey*, women still do approximately 30 percent[6] more housework and child care than their spouses. Even in homes where couples split chores like cooking, cleaning, laundry, and lawn care, women still shoulder the burden of invisible tasks like scheduling doctor's appointments, registering for camps, arranging carpools, and organizing playdates.

What's remained the same is that many women are still "rejecting the workforce," as Belkin wrote. They've peeked up at the top of the corporate ladder and they don't like what they see. In researching this book, I spoke with one hundred women, from all across the country, in all different professions and from all different stages of life, and, certainly, I met plenty of women who were fully engaged in their careers and striving for their next promotion. But for every one of those women, I met at least two who were content to fly under the radar at work or step off the track completely, and another who was conflicted about what she should do next.

The difference between the women I talked to and the women Belkin featured years ago is that the women I met can't easily opt out. The current economic climate just doesn't support women leaving the workforce. But life as a working mother is hard, really hard, and when women look at what work has to offer versus what home has to offer, many of them are choosing home. They're not quitting their jobs, necessarily; they're just scaling back. Women are looking at four-day workweeks, three-day workweeks, or positions that won't require more responsibility, longer hours, or travel.

The pressures of child rearing, coupled with a corporate culture that doesn't fulfill them in ways the women who went before them perhaps hoped it would, are too great to be ignored. And it's not just the most privileged women who are seeking a different course. Middle-class women with varying levels of education and ambition are scaling back, stopping at middle management, going through the motions, while they seek that elusive balance they crave.

Women's influence and power haven't changed much since Belkin published her article in 2003. Among the Fortune 500, women hold just 14.4 percent of executive officer positions and just 16.1 percent of all board seats. In terms of fair pay, the gender-based wage gap is currently stuck at 77 percent, and it's even greater for working mothers, who earn, on average, just 72.5 percent of what men earn.

I was particularly curious about what was happening at home that might be impeding women's advancement. There's a wealth of materials available that examine the workplace barriers women face and what can be done about them. But why was it that men seemed less encumbered by housework and child care? And what impact did that have on women at work? We can't do it all, especially when we're so busy doing the dishes. And besides, aren't men, like women, longing for more time with their families, more time to pursue interests other than work? Are women really better suited to stocking the pantry shelves, folding the items in the linen closet, and chauffeuring the kids than their husbands are?

The more I talked with women breadwinners, however, the more I realized I was asking the wrong question. It doesn't matter why the disparities exist as much as it matters what we do about them. How can women cope with the realities of modern breadwinning? What happens when women give up their goals and their earning potential to manage their households? How do women manage all the juggling, tension, and exhaustion? Are women rationalizing their decision to cut back at work as well as their spouse's decision not to, and at what cost? Some women assert that their actions have saved their marriage from failure. Others avow that dedicating themselves to their home life is more fulfilling than anything else they may have been doing. And many find a new home for their talents by pursuing a hobby, volunteering, or starting a work-from-home business.

It's important that women talk about these decisions. There was a scene in the first season of the popular prime-time drama *Desperate Housewives*, in which the wives find their friend Lynette in the middle of a soccer field crying about what a bad mother she thinks she is. Her friends comfort her by sharing their own insecurities and reassuring her they feel the same way. Relieved she is not alone, Lynette sobs, "Why didn't you ever tell me this? We should tell each other this stuff."

Sharing with other women, knowing we're not the only ones who are experiencing our feelings and challenges, is important. As we give voice to what is happening in our lives, we can address the challenges, make more informed decisions, and change what isn't working.

And changes are needed. A study from the London School of Economics showed divorce rates are lower in marriages where husbands help with housework. A Gallup Poll revealed that women who are full-time homemakers but want to be employed have an increased risk of depression. And beyond individual relationships and health, women's workforce participation has important implications for the economy, too, implications husbands should pay attention to, as well as CEOs and shareholders. According to the management consulting firm McKinsey & Company, women are a key to the United States sustaining its historic gross domestic product (GDP) growth rate of 3 percent. And it's been well documented in research from Catalyst and Credit Suisse that women improve both productivity and profits.

Mogul, Mom, & Maid: The Balancing Act of the Modern Woman builds on the stories of women navigating home life and work life and offers a way to move from conversation to action. We discuss negotiation as a critical career skill and how to use it at home as well as in the office. Some couples are getting it right; we hear from the women in those relationships as well, and learn how they arranged a healthy and equitable balance at home and at work. Some businesses are getting it right too. We look at what happens when companies become part of the solution, including offering house-cleaning services as a benefit to employees. At the conclusion of each chapter we share "Lessons from the Ladies," advice gleaned from the women interviewed for the book, as well as from my blog, Hello Ladies.

When we start talking about what's really going on inside the minds of today's breadwinners, we find new choices that support our spouses, our families, our employers, our economy, and most importantly, ourselves. *Mogul, Mom, & Maid: The Balancing Act of the Modern Woman* is less an advice book and more a cautionary tale—of why women are key to the future and what we must do to support their choices at home and at work.

1

Meet the New Breadwinner:
Part Mogul, Part Mom, Part Maid

I always knew I'd be a breadwinner. Maybe not the sole bread-winner, but I knew I'd work. When I was growing up in the 1970s, one of my childhood fantasies was that I'd have a dual career—surgeon during the week and Hollywood actress on the weekends. And when reality got in the way of that daydream—I hate the sight of blood and I suffer from stage fright—I started building my corporate empire in my head. I called it Unicorn Enterprises, and I had a crystal-clear image of the company logo. Unicorn Enterprises was going to be a holding company for many different ventures: a newspaper, a retail chain, and a few more businesses I can no longer remember. My parents indulged my dreams. I don't know if it was the feminist influences of the time, their desire for their daughter to achieve more than they did, or my straight As in school, but both of them, and especially my father, wanted me to pursue a "good job," aka a high-paying career, when I grew up.

Back then I didn't give any thought to work–life balance. For, while I daydreamed about my high-powered career choices, I also played house, for hours and hours, with my best friend, Stephanie, who lived next door. Her grandmother crocheted blankets and booties for our dolls and we'd swaddle them, then take them for walks up and down the street in toy carriages. We'd pretend to take our babies to the park in the morning and then stop by our imaginary kids' school at lunchtime, just like our own moms, who were both lunchroom volunteers and PTA members. I remember thinking the ultimate mom would surprise her kids with a meal from McDonald's delivered to the school every now and then. Boy, was I off base. It never occurred to me that the CEO of an international conglomerate like Unicorn Enterprises couldn't be a classroom volunteer, never mind that feeding a child McDonald's is the badge of a bad mother, not a supermom, to my generation.

Today I'm not a CEO, nor am I affiliated with Unicorn Enterprises, which appears to be a privately held computer company in Switzerland. But I am a mother who feeds her kids McDonald's meals occasionally, and I am the breadwinner for my family—the sole breadwinner in fact. It's an arrangement my husband and I discussed early in our marriage, well before we had children. As a result, the only long walks with baby carriages I've ever taken were during my short maternity leaves or on weekends. And while I do occasionally volunteer at my children's school, I never stop by at lunchtime. I can't. I'm thirty minutes away by train, most likely eating at my desk.

The Rise of the Breadwinner

As a sole-breadwinning, married mother, I belong to a small but growing group. The Bureau of Labor Statistics reports just 8 percent of American families rely exclusively on a woman's salary.[1] But as the primary breadwinner, I have more company. Close to 40 percent of U.S. working wives now outearn their husbands, with Bureau of Labor Statistics data revealing that in married-couple families where both the husband and wife receive a paycheck, 28.1 percent of the wives earn more than their husbands.[2] And even though the mainstream media might lead you to believe all women are real housewives, and that mothers in a modern family are omnipresent in their children's lives, the majority of mothers work outside the home. So I've actually got plenty of company when you include me with the women who contribute some of the family income and are therefore at least partial breadwinners. Based on the same Bureau of Labor Statistics data, mothers are employed in 65.4 percent of married-couple families,[3] contributing at least some of the family income.

It makes sense. Women have the means: we've been outnumbering men on college campuses for years and outpacing them when it comes to graduate degrees. We have the desire. A study from the Center for Work–Life Policy showed that at the start of their careers, 47 percent of young women claim to be "very ambitious." And we have the need. Women's participation in the labor force increased just over a percentage point since the start of the recession.[4] Today's women are working for much more than power and fulfillment. They're paying the mortgage, the grocery bills, and the medical benefits. And if the rise in female breadwinners continues at the same pace it has in recent years, it's likely that in just a few years more families will be supported by women than by men.

The Myth of the Female Breadwinner

In recent years, there's been a slew of articles and research dedicated to the female breadwinner. We've been treated almost like mythical beings to be studied and figured out— you'd think we'd be better understood, as there are more than twenty-three million working mothers in this country.[5] A *Wall Street Journal* article from July 2012 referred to the dynamic between female breadwinners and their spouses as the alpha woman versus beta male. *Elle* magazine, a few months earlier, was even more colorful, talking about how female "hunters" felt about "the stay-at-home schlub." And last year, *New York* magazine ran a feature story, a cautionary tale, about how breadwinning wives' "new financial muscle is causing havoc in the home." According to author Ralph Gardner Jr., shell-shocked husbands feel emasculated by their alpha wives.

I interviewed working women all over the country, at many different stages in their careers, in many different industries—not one of them mentioned a shell-shocked schlub—and what I found is that their feelings about working and family are incredibly layered. One night, over a few glasses of wine in the living room of a neighbor who is a research consultant, I spoke with six women, five of them the majority breadwinners for their families. These women were tired and busy, certainly, but they were comfortable in their own skin, were accepting of their roles, and expressed no mothering guilt—another common working-women narrative in the mainstream media. The only niggling concern several of them shared was their lack of freedom to pursue different career choices, mission-based work, as they described it, that might feed their souls more but pay them less than what they were currently earning. But all of them felt it was their own choices that had landed them in the breadwinner role, and I sensed no resentment. One woman, a doctor who owns a private practice, even hinted at the frequency of sex she and her husband, a teacher, have. A recent intimate moment had taken place after her husband cleaned the dirty dinner pans that were her assigned responsibility one night.

The doctor better fits the description of the female breadwinner in Liza Mundy's book *The Richer Sex: How the New Majority of Female Breadwinners Is Transforming Sex, Love and Family,* than she does the one in Gardner's article. Mundy paints a much brighter future for breadwinning women and their spouses. She writes that ultimately women will have "the bargaining power they need to usher in a new age of fairness, complete the revolution, push us past the unhappy days of the so-called second shift, when so many men and women were mired in arguments over equity that always seemed to boil down to laundry and dishes." Hopefully, she's right. But first, some changes need to be made.

The Breadwinner's Reality

The reality of working women lies somewhere between Gardner and Mundy. There is no one standard profile of a female breadwinner; the lives of modern working women are complex, and their path to becoming the breadwinner is rarely as they'd planned—in fact, it's highly likely it was never planned at all.

For starters, it's the rare woman over the age of thirty who seriously considered work–life balance before she began her career or her family. Like me, she may have played with dolls, but it's doubtful she sent them to pretend day care. Growing up, she most likely saw two iconic images of working mothers on prime-time television. The spokesmodel in an Enjoli perfume ad told us she could, "bring home the bacon, fry it up in a pan, and never, never, never let you forget you're a man." She could also, "put the wash on the line, feed the kids, get dressed, pass out the kisses and get to work by five to nine." The other image—fictitious, high-octane Clair Huxtable from the *Cosby Show*—struggled on screen sometimes trying to manage five children and a job as an attorney, but still we wanted what she had: well-adjusted kids, a supportive and loving husband, an impeccable house, and a meaningful career. Through the mainstream media we received the message we could have it all, and we believed it.

Lately, there's been considerable debate about whether or not a woman can have it all, and a Princeton University professor named Anne-Marie Slaughter has fueled much of it. In an article she published in the July 2012 issue of *The Atlantic*, titled "Why Women Still Can't Have It All," Slaughter publicly confessed she was opting out of a high-powered position in the State Department working for then–Secretary of State Hillary Clinton, because she didn't think she could juggle a power position and two teenage boys. Hidden in Slaughter's story is something many women hadn't considered—it's not just mothering infants and toddlers that can cause a woman's career to veer off course, it's parenting teens, and caring for aging parents too.

Maybe Babies Are the Easy Part

Even if our childhood imaginary play didn't involve balancing our boss's needs with our children's needs, certainly by the time we started our first jobs out of high school or college we were well aware that new mothers often struggle at work. Parenting books and magazines are full of the pitfalls—short maternity leaves, breastfeeding challenges, sleepless nights, and day-care schedules. And so many of us, perhaps desperate to believe things would get easier, bought into a tacit belief that once the kids hit elementary school, work–life balance would become more manageable. That's not necessarily the case.

As Slaughter discovered and several mothers have told me, the middle school years introduce a whole new parenting dynamic that's written about much less than the challenges of working while parenting infants. For example, middle school is often when the after-school programs that many working mothers depend on end. "What is she going to do after school?" one mother, whose daughter had just left elementary school, asked. "That's when it gets important that you're home." In middle school, children are usually introduced to a broader set of peers, their interests and activities change, and, while they may not need as much physical support from their parents, they often need extra emotional support. Another mother, the director of development for a nonprofit, lamented that, as a working mother, it can be difficult to meet the parents and families of your child's new friends. Most working mothers would say it's a challenge to meet people in their communities any time, but at least when your children are younger, the odds of meeting other parents at the playground or on a school field trip are higher.

And then there are our parents. An AARP report finds the average caregiver for elderly parents is a forty-nine-year-old working woman. But, despite the fact that these caregivers represent an estimated 15 to 25 percent of the workforce, the Society for Human Resource Management reports there has been a decrease in the number of companies that provide assistance to employees in the form of eldercare programs. And caregiving can take a major toll on a career. According to a study by the Working Mother Research Institute, caregiving women feel judged by coworkers, unable to accept promotions, and challenged trying to manage their job responsibilities. Often, a working mother's time out of the office during her childbearing years is compounded by the time off she takes later to care for her parents. And just like the little girl I once was, pretending to be a mogul and a mom, many, if not most, of today's female breadwinners never planned how they would balance all of these family obligations and a career—they just expected they could have it all.

Women Carry the Laundry Load

If having it all means having responsibility for earning a paycheck, raising children, caring for family members, and managing a household, then indeed, most working mothers can claim they've got it. The Census Bureau's *American Time Use Survey* shows men are doing more at home than ever before, doubling their share of housework and tripling their share of child care. But even with the increase, women still do approximately 30 percent more housework and child care than their spouses. And in homes where couples evenly split chores like cooking, cleaning, laundry, and lawn care, it's usually the women who shoulder the burden of invisible tasks like scheduling doctor's appointments, registering for camps, arranging car pools, and organizing playdates. These invisible chores take up as much mental focus and energy as the physical tasks. "I do all the laundry," says Sharon, an MBA who works as an analyst in an investment firm. "It's not just the laundry, it's the mental awareness of the laundry. I know my son has only seven pairs of pants. I know it's swimming day on Tuesday. I think through if his swimming stuff is packed up, including the swim cap. It's the small details. And anything related to a doctor's appointment, dentist, birthday parties, playdates, car pools, that's me." Sharon's husband, a software developer, helps by dropping off and picking up the kids at school and by driving the car pool. But it's Sharon who organizes the car-pool schedule.

Something's Got to Give

Between the current economic climate, the structure of the American family, and the demands of the workplace, we are asking today's women to do more than ever before. Some are soldiering on, trying to make it all work, and others are saying it's too much, that something's got to give.

In 2003, Lisa Belkin wrote a *New York Times* article titled "The Opt-Out Revolution," in which she profiled successful, educated women who were "rejecting the workplace." Critics said Belkin's subjects were privileged women who could afford to stop working; they said the same thing about Slaughter. But a good number of the women I spoke with either want to cut back at work or already have. Some of them could more easily afford to do that than others, and those who were less affluent decided the financial sacrifices were worth the personal rewards.

I asked women who left corporate America in favor of part-time work, an entrepreneurial endeavor, a consulting gig, or staying at home full time why they made that choice, and very often they cited the challenge of managing a career and a household as one of the main reasons. I asked them how their husbands managed career and home, and they told me that was a different story.

Under the veil of anonymity, one woman told me her decision to leave her job as the executive director of a state agency after the birth of her child led to a personal crisis. "I was really angry at my husband. His job required sacrifice from me, but mine didn't require sacrifice from him." She struggled with the decision until her marriage counselor told her, "You have to quit your job." Another woman told me, "Women aren't going to be honest [about this topic]." She too left an executive position to focus on her family. "It was clear in our current setup that the role of the home falls on me."

But most of the women I spoke with were simply resigned to carrying more than their fair share at home. "Women and men are just different," they told me. "Women care more about order and cleanliness. Women are more organized. Women can multitask." The women I spoke with were less concerned with why household responsibilities break down the way they do and more concerned with what to do about it. What some of these women go through to manage everything and get it all done could break your heart.

"I get up at 5:15, get to work at 9, and I'm thoroughly exhausted by that time," says Linda, a regional business manager and chief of staff at a commercial bank. "I have been up, made lunch, woken the kids, thrown in laundry. And we don't make beds. They get made every two weeks. It feels like Groundhog Day; I do the same thing over and over again. You can push hard through something but when you don't see the end of it, it's torture." This same woman described her nighttime routine as equally grueling: "I leave at 4:30, but I work at night. The kids go to bed at 8:30 and I will work until midnight."

It's no wonder these breadwinners feel pulled in too many directions. "I feel like I suck as an employee, suck as a mom, suck as a wife," says Linda. "There are not enough hours in a day to do all three of them, or any of them, well. I wonder where I'd be in my career if I didn't have a family. And I wonder how much better behaved my kids would be if I didn't work?"

Where's the ROI?

When faced with the choice of doing an average job at many things or excelling at a few, many women choose their priorities based on what has the highest return on investment. And for many women creating a positive environment for their families yields a greater return than creating profit for shareholders, especially when you consider women still face many barriers to success and satisfaction at work.

Women are making slow, if any, progress toward breaking the glass ceiling to access the top positions at work. Despite the fact that women represent almost half of today's workforce, among the Fortune 500 they hold just 16.6 percent of board seats and just 14.3 percent of executive officer positions, according to the Catalyst *2012 F500 Census*, which annually tracks women in top corporate positions. Too few companies have adopted family-friendly policies such as mentoring programs, flexible schedules, better child care, and telecommuting programs that make work life manageable. The United States is one of only four countries that doesn't offer paid maternity leave, so almost half of all women end up stringing together sick days, vacation days, disability leave, and whatever maternity leave their employers offer. When the women return to work they might find themselves pumping breast milk in an electrical closet full of spiders like I did or in a garage at the courthouse like Kelly, a divorce attorney, did. Then, if and when their children get sick, the working mother will most likely need to call in sick too—unless she is one of the 4 percent of Americans whose employer offers back-up child care[6] and as long she isn't one of the 48 percent of workers in the private sector who doesn't receive any paid sick days.[7]

And there is the issue of the wage gap, which shows no signs of shrinking. In 2011, the median earnings of women who worked full time, year-round were 77 percent of that for men working full time, year-round. For women of color, the gap is even larger. The *Journal of Contemporary Economic Policy* concluded that each hour of housework reduces women's wages by 0.1 to 0.4 percent. Researchers Joni Hersch and Leslie S. Stratton studied data from the *Panel Study of Income Dynamics* revealing a substantial negative correlation between wages and housework for wives. In the *Journal of Human Resources*, they suggested one theory for this could be employers' negative reactions to women who appear dedicated to household activities.

The Mommy Penalty Is Real

On top of the gender-based pay gap, women's wages are threatened by the "mommy penalty." A report published by the University of Chicago Press highlights two studies that show that employed mothers in the United States suffer a per-child wage penalty of approximately 5 percent, on average, and for women under the age of thirty-five, the pay gap between mothers and non-mothers is larger than the pay gap between men and women.

When you consider the demands and responsibilities of a woman's home life, you see why she might choose to opt out, or at least scale back. When you marry those responsibilities with the hurdles and barriers she encounters at work, you have to consider whether she's being pushed out, instead of jumping.

Why We Need Women at Work

Regardless of whether women are jumping or being pushed, it behooves us all to ensure that more women are set up to succeed at work and at home. According to the management consulting firm McKinsey & Company, in order for the United States to sustain its historic gross domestic product (GDP) growth rate of 3 percent, we need to expand the workforce and increase productivity. Women are key to both. If the U.S. could increase to 84 percent the workplace participation rate of women in each state, it would add 5.1 million women, which is the equivalent of 3 or 4 percent GDP growth. Highly skilled women who have opted out or scaled back could be the answer to positions left unfilled by employers who can't match jobs with qualified employees.

Women at work don't just improve productivity, they also improve profits. A nineteen-year study of 215 Fortune 500 firms showed a solid correlation between a strong record of promoting women into the executive suite and high profitability. Fortune 500 firms with the best record of promoting women to high positions were between 18 and 69 percent more profitable than the median Fortune 500 firms in the same industries. Additional data from McKinsey shows companies with three or more women in senior management functions perform better on average than companies without a critical mass of women.

Why Mom Should Go to Work

Families benefit from women working at the highest levels too. Experts calculate that the wage gap translates into approximately $10,000 less per year in median earnings for women when compared with men. With more than half of American women who work contributing at least some part of the necessary income to maintain their households, it's imperative that we close this gap and help women access the top salaries. Mortgages, grocery bills, child care expenditures, school fees, and medical bills are dependent on women earning their fair share. In other words, our country's economic health depends on women and men working together in the office and at home.

The good news is women are resourceful. This fact was borne out in my conversations with scores of working women: they manage to raise kids, run homes, volunteer, and go to work—all at the same time. They take on the added responsibility of caring for aging family members when their schedules are already overbooked. They figure out how to survive in corporate settings where the odds are stacked against them. They know how to tap into a deep well of optimism and fortitude in order to get things done. Making the dinner and managing the household finances aren't going to stand in the way of their goals.

What follows are the real-life stories of today's women, although some names have been changed to protect the women's privacy. By listening to their voices, we can glean important lessons about how all of us—spouses, friends, employers and legislators—can best support these forces of nature so that they can continue to do what they do best: all of it.

I'll start with one of my own stories, and I'll share more with you throughout the book. This first story is about one morning in the life of this working mother.

So this morning I was running late for work because I had a hard time picking out an outfit because last Saturday I forgot to go to the dry cleaner because I was really busy shuffling my kids from soccer practice to the town-wide barbecue birthday bash to a party we were all invited to and so I had no clean work pants and I couldn't wear knee-length skirts or capris because I was gardening on Sunday because I hadn't weeded since June because every weekend in the summer I took my kids to the Cape so they could hang out with their cousins and anyway I got poison ivy on my legs and therefore hadn't shaved them all week but I had to dress professionally because my boss and I were going to an industry event later in the day to network with potential clients.

So, I decided to wear a long, flowy, black skirt, and after trying many different tops finally paired it with a black cardigan that looked professional and put on a pair of low black heels that wouldn't hurt walking around a trade show floor and I threw on some appropriate accessories and I was ready to go but I stopped to use the bathroom because I have a long commute and I had downed three cups of coffee and…the back of my skirt fell in the toilet!

So, I had a meltdown and started ranting and my husband said, "How is this my fault?" to which I responded, "It's not your fault. Why can't I get upset without you thinking you need to fix it?" at which point my nine-year-old son came up to me, hugged me, and said, "I love you, Mom," which, while really sweet, made me realize he was trying to calm down psycho-mommy and someday he'd be in therapy because of me.

Then I went upstairs and I found a long skirt (linen, which, I don't care what *Vogue* says, is a no-no after Labor Day in New England), which really needed ironing but I decided not to iron because it was just going to be wrinkled again by the time I got to work and as I pulled it out of the closet the button popped off and it required a new top and new shoes because it was brown not black and I didn't really have a top that matched except the sweater I had worn to the party Saturday which I couldn't find because my house is always a mess.

And so I ran around trying to find a top and praying to St. Anthony to find my sweater and my hair started to frizz because the weather was really humid because September is always warmer than August in New England, which is Mother Nature's way of messing with working parents who have to take the last week in August as vacation because that's the week between when camp ends and school starts and I couldn't pull my hair back because my daughter, in the middle of all this, asked me for a ponytail holder even though she always takes mine and should have had a bazillion of them and where the hell do they go and my husband pointed out I have a bunch of them in my office but I didn't want my daughter to go in there because Sunday night I was sorting though my vintage necklaces in the office because it relaxes me but I got interrupted and never put them away and they were still on the floor and I didn't want her to step on them, so I gave her the one I always keep on my wrist.

So my hair was wild and I had nothing to wear except a wrinkly linen skirt until I noticed a shirt I bought at the Gap and had planned to return because I spent too much money last time I was there but it was desperate times so I put it on but it still required a cardigan so that didn't really help because St. Anthony wasn't listening so I grabbed another Gap shirt out of my closet as I realized I still had to keep the new shirt because I had removed the tags and tossed it on the floor and it would be wrinkled by the time I got home.

I glanced in the mirror at my wild hair and casual outfit and saw I was not even close to the look-at-me-I'm-large-and-in-charge-trust-me-with-your-communications-strategy image I wanted to project at the event but I had no choice but to wear the outfit so I decided to channel Iris Apfel and added a multistrand turquoise necklace and leopard shoes and hoped I could project a look-at-me-I'm-hip-and-creative-trust-me-with-your-social-media-strategy image even though I knew I couldn't because I'm a middle-aged suburban mother.

And as I went to finally leave, I realized I needed to change bags because now the big, printed bag I had planned to carry was too casual whereas before it had served as a pop of color for an all-black outfit and so I wanted to grab a more structured purse but I couldn't fit my flats (also leopard) in the structured bag and there was no way I was going to a trade show without back-up flats and so I finally found an appropriate bag but that necessitated transferring my wallet, lunch, sunglasses, and cosmetics to another bag, which was risky business because it had to be done on the go and I couldn't really risk any erratic or distracted driving because I had no registration or inspection sticker because my leasing company had sent the paperwork late and I was supposed to go the RMV and get that sorted out at lunch but how could I leave work for a few hours to do that when I was going to arrive so late?

Then when I got in the car I realized it was on empty because I hadn't stopped for gas the night before because I wanted to get home before it got too dark to go for a run because running helps my stress levels and I hadn't run Tuesday night because I went to the PTO meeting which was painful—I mean I appreciate all the board does, but ladies, really, *Robert's Rules of Order*, live it, learn it, love it—and I didn't run on Monday night because I was at an environmental committee meeting because I need to save the world and I was having a hard time waking up in the mornings to run ever since school started because my daughter, who is exhausted readjusting to a schedule after sleeping late all summer, had been throwing temper tantrums at night and I had been giving in and lying down with her even though I knew I was reinforcing bad behavior and I think seven is too old for the Ferber method and her crying and whining was reminding me of when she was a baby and I had postpartum depression and I just wanted her to go to sleep.

When I finished pumping gas a woman with a sleek chignon and cool sunglasses dressed very professionally pulled in and blocked me at the gas tank and I thought, if she is a working mother and looks that good she deserves to have her suit dunked in the toilet, but I finally got out of there without incident and tuned in to the traffic report and heard there was an accident and not one, but two lanes, were blocked on the highway and then I remembered I had thrown the black skirt into the laundry and it's dry-clean only, which meant either my husband was going to a) wash it as a nice gesture and accidentally ruin it or b) not wash it which would piss me off because wasn't that the least he could do?

And then, as I sat in the traffic jam thinking about how I wasn't going to get to work until practically tomorrow, which was really a problem because I was behind on some things because I'd been spending a lot of time on one specific project, which ironically had to do with how mothers "do it all," which meant I would either have to work late and skip another run or get caught up on work on the weekend therefore not having any time to go to the dry cleaner, I turned on the air conditioner because my hair kept frizzing from the heat and I realized I had worn my office sweater home the night before, which could have been a problem because my coworker always blasts the AC at the office because she's in menopause and having hot flashes and who am I to judge because that could be me, like, tomorrow and because the fabric on my shirt was really thin it would be revealing, if you know what I mean, but luckily Rachel Zoe has nothing on me and I could fix the problem with Band-Aids.

And, inspired by my many talents I decided to write this— while driving—because I downloaded the speech-to-text software on my iPhone one day while imagining I could be that kind of supermom who multitasks and has all the right apps, which, according to a new study, makes me prone to depression (the wanting to be a supermom, not the apps) but I never did get around to downloading the app that reads e-mails aloud, which would have been useful because at that point I was already forty-five minutes late for work and not yet at the halfway mark and I was only driving twenty-five miles an hour even though I had already passed the accident.

And that is the life of a working mother.

LESSONS FROM THE LADIES

WOMEN:

- Think about balance when planning your career. Every life choice has consequences and requires tradeoffs.
- Ignore the media hype and choose the lifestyle that works for you and your family.
- Remember motherhood is a lifetime experience that extends beyond the infant and toddler phase.
- Build your village when your children are young; it's harder to meet other families when your children are in middle school and high school.

EMPLOYERS:

- Consider eldercare assistance for employees with caregiving responsibilities.
- Examine work/life policies that help parents balance career and family.

2

A Perfect Storm:
The Working Mother's Struggle

In 1976, Sally graduated from college and married her boyfriend, Neil. Neil got a job in New England with a Fortune 500 company and Sally got a job as the first female salesperson for a well-established tabletop company. "I traveled the states of Maine, New Hampshire, and Vermont. At that time, there were no women on the road, yet the product was geared to women—it was all about women. I loved the product and loved to travel."

Sally did all the laundry, cooking, and grocery shopping for herself and Neil. "I wasn't resentful," she says. "I could work out of my house. I didn't have an office. I traveled or stayed home where I could do paperwork." Sally was named Salesman of the Year twice. "The superwoman," she says.

Eventually, the couple moved to the Southwest. "We were fighting over the cleaning and the cooking. The housework, we tried to divide up. It was such a bone of contention. We said, 'We're going to get help or our marriage will suffer.' We had a two-bedroom flat. It was extravagant, but since then we've never been without [cleaning] help. Psychologically, to walk into a house that smells of Pine-Sol and see the dust gone, it's incredibly lifting to your spirit."

Ten years into her career and now working for a competitor, Sally had her first child, a daughter they named Melissa. "I'm still traveling half of Texas, New Mexico. I attended trade shows in New York four times per year. We got help that took care of Melissa but the nightmare of scheduling…"

Sally managed the schedule—when she was traveling, when Neil was traveling, when they needed child care. "It was this extra layer of work," Sally said. "I didn't know about a spreadsheet. Some mornings I'd leave the house at 5:00 a.m. I'd coordinate my schedule with Neil's work. Did I need to fly back home?"

On top of the scheduling, Sally booked all of her own travel. She and Neil had a second child, a son, and a babysitter who didn't drive, so Sally enlisted a friend who was a taxi driver to pick up Melissa at preschool. "The anxiety around that, to know that your child is being picked up. The cabbie would be late—fifteen minutes. We were fined and then kicked out of the school."

A Primal Duty to Feed?

Despite her full-time job and busy schedule, Sally said she was the one in the marriage who took the children to doctor's appointments and stayed home when they were sick. "I had a therapist who told me it was my duty to feed the children. I was complaining that since my husband worked and I worked and we both made equal money why should I have to be responsible for all the child care? She said that I fed and nourished the baby in utero so it was still my primal duty to feed and care for them. She said, 'I don't care if you drive through McDonald's and get a Happy Meal. You bring it home and put it on a plate and feed your children.' I certainly bought into it."

Almost instinctively, Sally created her own flex schedule. "I didn't have to lie or take vacation days. I was living in the epicenter of the retail world, so I could get home and then get back to my appointments. It worked pretty well but it was still pretty crazy. I remember sitting in appointments with Melissa in a Snugli."

As hard as it was to manage work, family, and a household, Sally liked working and wanted to continue. "I was making big money. I had really good child care. I had women who doted on my children, and my kids were taken care of so well. And I believed if I was home and took them to soccer and games… I killed myself to be home at night. But when my son was four and Melissa was seven, it became evident they needed me at home. I had worked eighteen years. I was anemic. I was doing the supermom thing. I quit and never looked back."

Sally says she regrets she didn't spend the formative years with her kids but she was so happy working. "At the time, yeah, I think it was hard. With a little more maturity I see I should have asked for help. It was just those times."

Sally only knew two other women who worked, and she had no role models. "I was making it up; I didn't know what to expect. I was always with men. I didn't know there was any other way."

Same Story, Different Decade

Today's working women have more role models and peers than Sally did, but do we really know what to expect either? Are we ever truly prepared for what it's like to have both a career and a family? And are our stories, so many years later, very different from Sally's? Women today still struggle with feelings of isolation at work and at home, and with worrying about what to feed their children and who's going to pick them up on time from school. We still wrestle with whose career comes first, ours or our spouse's, who should pay for dinner and who should make it. One could argue that today's working women have it harder than Sally and her few peers did. We're no longer trailblazers, but we still don't know where we fit. And so we find ourselves making up the rules as we go.

Kate Davis, a nonprofit fund-raiser, and her husband both work full time and earn approximately the same salary. "It's always a struggle," she says. "In the past, whoever made a little less had to bend a little. You have to play that whose-job-is-more-important game. It's a strain."

The Perfect Storm

Meteorologists use the term "perfect storm" to describe a critical situation created by a powerful concurrence of factors. That's what women like Kate face every day. The challenges of building and managing a career, coordinating with a spouse's career, the responsibilities of raising a family, plus the demands of outside influences—including extended family, friends, schools, and, if you can swing it, personal interests—create a pressure system to rival even the greatest weather events. And, just like weather-related tempests, these events can leave damage in their wake if you're not prepared for them.

Women are two times more likely than men to suffer from depression. And married women experience depression at a higher rate than single women, according to the National Institutes of Mental Health (NIMH). Women also suffer higher rates of anxiety than men. In an interview with NBC News, anxiety researcher Jean Twenge, PhD, said, "Recent generations have been told over and over again, 'You can be anything you want to be. You can have the big job title. You can have the big bank account'...That puts a lot on a person's shoulders—and it's also not really true. These are things that aren't always under your control, but that disconnect creates a lot of anxiety about how hard you need to work to achieve them."

Where Are the Part-Time Options?

Like Kate, Shana Ross is a nonprofit fund-raiser, however she works part time. And she, too, had to make choices about whose career—hers or her psychiatrist husband's—would take priority following the birth of her now eighteen-month-old son. Shana says, "When we decided to have kids, we talked about who should really focus on career at this point in our lives. It made sense that I quit what I was doing, so I opened up my own consultancy. I really restructure my life and my career when I need to, and guess what? It happens all the time because toddlers get sick."

Shana's previous job had required frequent travel to meet with donors, and she described the hours as ridiculous. "I didn't want that competing with my child." But she would like to be doing meaningful, high-paying work with the time she can commit. Despite the fact she has an MBA, Shana finds there are too few career opportunities for what she calls women in the middle: "I'm looking for a high-powered, part-time job, and those don't really exist. And it's not to say my husband hasn't shifted his career schedule around, having a kid. I do more child care but he has picked up more housework. And it's not like he hasn't made similar sacrifices. They just look different. I am someone who's invested a lot in a career. It's a little pathologic for me. I grew up with an abusive father who never worked and a mother who supported the family but never broke away. It's very important for me to support myself if I have to. I grew up on welfare and eating out of food pantries; the fact I can support myself—that I am always conscious of. My pet peeve is the lack of real options for women of my caliber. Let's be clear. Full-time is not forty hours a week. Full-time is sixty to eighty hours a week for folks with higher degrees. Where is the option for women who don't want that?"

Meghan also wants to work, despite her original plan to stay home after she and her husband of twelve years started a family. The couple has an eight-year-old and a six-year-old, and Meghan was home with the children until 2009, when her husband lost his job. "The plan was I would stay home—that's what I wanted. I never wanted to put my kids on the bus and rush off. But when my husband lost his job, it was like something has to give."

Meghan's husband opened an auto body repair shop after he was laid off, and she found work as a freelance writer, working full time out of the house and overseeing the books for the repair shop. "It's going okay, but we make well less than half of what he brought home before the layoff. I'm now able to work full time from home, but really have to hustle to make enough to cover our household bills."

Balancing Career and Marriage

Meghan's new full-time status has put a strain on the family and the marriage. "The balance between my career and my marriage is precarious," she says. "The house doesn't get or stay clean and the clean laundry is usually piled high. I cook dinner, but sometimes it's leftovers or frozen dinners. He hates coming home to a cluttered and untidy house. He knows I need to work and he does help clean up, but I still feel tension because I'm not doing more. I'm not sitting around all day playing computer games. I'm homeschooling our youngest and I'm working. Yet I'm also expected to clean, cook, grocery shop, pay bills. I do the laundry. There have been times I have not gotten to his wash and he gets really perturbed because he needs clean clothes for work. Then I feel guilty. I do 95 percent of the cooking; he might make his own sandwich. Cleaning is fifty-fifty. Errands are all me. Grocery shopping is all me.

"Part of our problem is the old-school train of thought—a woman works at home so her man doesn't have to. I'm blessed with a husband who helps, but I sense he does that because he's exasperated by the house, not because he loves me or supports my career. I always tell myself I'll do better at balancing work and home, but work always wins. Everything is half done. The dishes are clean but not put away. The laundry is clean but not put away. I think he thinks it's my choice. I think he thinks I want to be working all the time. I don't have a social life, don't sleep. I've threatened to cut back on work, but we barely survive as it is. He's talked about getting another job so I can work less, but the job market gives no guarantees that he'll get hired or make enough. Plus, we'd need a second car at an additional expense if he got a different job."

And the truth is, Meghan likes earning a paycheck. "Now that I'm working, I'm really grateful for it. It's really invigorating to know someone wants my services. I want to do this for the rest of my life. Part of the strategy with my writing business is—my husband is older. What if something happens to him? My career is like life insurance.

"I think most women have this innate desire to be the nurturer and take care of the children," Meghan says. "It's just, there are two parents. If husbands aren't making enough… and that's the thing that really gets me, when people say you're wrong for wanting to work or you're wrong for wanting to stay home. Let's be nice to each other."

Pumping in the Parking Lot

Kelly, the divorce attorney who pumped breast milk in a court garage, isn't concerned about traditional gender roles. Her husband is a stay-at-home dad who bartends two days a week. They have a child under the age of one and another on the way. His staying home with the kids was always the plan, she says. "He works cause he likes it; it makes him feel better. He worked a lot more [when we met] but he cut back when we were married just so we could see each other."

While Kelly is comfortable with the roles she and her husband have established at home, she faces obstacles at work as a female breadwinner. When I interviewed her she was working for a really small firm, with just four female attorneys. "Working for a small firm and having a baby is tough," Kelly says. "There is no paid maternity leave. I pumped for seven months.

Two or three weeks after I was back from maternity leave I did a four-day trial. I'd nurse, get to court by eight, pump in the bathroom with a shitty battery, deal with crazy counsel. Usually by noon, I got a break. Eight to twelve was a long time for me to go [without pumping]. I'd beg the probate secretaries to use their bathroom because they had an outlet and a lock. Then after lunch I'd pump in the parking lot, drive home in two-hour traffic and get home by 6:15."

Kelly's daughter was still getting up at night to nurse. And Kelly was tired. "But I didn't want to cut that out so that she'd drink less during the day. I worked for women who didn't breastfeed their children. It was kind of like this atmosphere of, it wasn't a big deal for me so it's not a big deal for you."

One of the reasons Kelly started her own firm was so she wouldn't have to explain her choices. "Are you coming back? That question always just annoyed me. Other women who work would ask me if I would work if I didn't have to. The first week I went back to work, I felt like the best mother I had been. I was patient, I had energy, I wanted to get on the floor and play. I didn't feel that way before. To this day, I still feel that way, although I'd like to work a little less. I look at the stuff Tom does, like the laundry, and the dishes, just day after day and week after week and I'm just so glad I'm not doing it."

But figuring out the family dynamic took some effort. "It was a process that had some really ugly heads to it. And some of it was when I was pregnant and I was really hormonal and I really lost my shit. 'Why cant you do laundry? We're going to have a baby and I'm going to work all week and come home and do laundry?' There were a couple of blowouts but I can't remember any blowouts since Molly was born."

She credits the more peaceful existence to the fact that she knows what her husband's days are like. "I also remember being on maternity leave, and, yeah, she napped all day but I needed to sit down and have a goddamn cup of coffee. So I think working mothers have to have a lot more sensitivity to what goes on in their home when they're gone. If our house is a mess, it's a mess. There's just so much to do at home; I don't think there's any way it could be compartmentalized that one who works only works and the one who stays home only does housekeeping."

Will She Know I Love Her?

Kelly is happy with her decision to be the breadwinner, has been successful enough to start her own private practice, and has formed a strong partnership with her husband. Still, she's not immune to doubts about her role as a mother: "I think the one thing that I worry about...or I don't even know if worrying is the right word...I want to make sure that Molly knows...and maybe working dads feel this way too...I just want Molly to know that I love her as much as her dad does even though I'm not here all the time. She and Tom have their own special rhythm. On weekends I put her down for her nap because I do worry a little bit about feeling left out. There's an expectation that babies need their mothers, and mommies are the ones that make it better. I'm the mom but Tom can make her stop crying faster than I can. So those thoughts creep in and then I go in the room in the morning and I see my kid grinning six ways 'til Sunday, and I don't worry."

In the HOV Lane, Alone

Just like Sally twenty to thirty years before us, women today are still caught between two competing identities: career woman and mother. Kim is an HR executive and a divorced mother of two. She's proud of the fact she was able to thrive postdivorce, and says her proudest moment was when she refinanced her house in her own name. Kim's created a life she loves, but she'll be the first to tell you just how hard it is. "I love my kids. I have this great second act. I'm from a long lineage of only children.

I never thought I'd have two, now all of a sudden…And I'm not that paranoid first-time mom. I let everything go. I have a demanding boss. I don't love my job but I love the money. I wish it could be a little less work. I'm always running around half-cocked."

Kim and I met at a mutual acquaintance's house one night after work, along with eight other women, to talk about the challenges of managing career and family. It wasn't easy for Kim to get there; she drove solo in the HOV lane in order to be on time. "Tonight, I booked it home; the baby was about to fall asleep. I'm saying, 'Please don't put her to bed.' I went in, read her a story, gave her a bottle, put on some blush, and went out."

Time management isn't her only challenge. Kim also feels torn between competing responsibilities—work and children—and caught between two worlds—that of the working mother and that of the stay-at-home mother. "I feel like there's this weird stay-at-home versus working mom thing," she says. "I have an obsession of looking into the world of the stay-at-home mother. I work with some senior men whose wives stay at home, and I think, 'How do you get that job to stay home and call your husband all day and ask him questions?' I'm intrigued by them and I hate them at the same time.

"I worked from home the other day and I took my daughter to Music Together. People were like, 'Oh are you the aunt?' I got [attitude] about it. Then I had all these conference calls; it's amazing what you have to do in the course of the day. I was so exhausted, totally wiped out, and I felt paranoid the next day, like people were judging me. Was I really working? But I was really working. I think the guilt and the paranoia—that's a constant part of it. Yesterday, all day, I was looking at my e-mail. I literally said out loud, 'Be present in the moment now. I'm working from home—just enjoy that one day.' And I couldn't."

Other women have also told me about the isolation they feel compared with other mothers, especially the ones they perceive as having a stronger social network. "I found it harder to meet people with younger kids," said a woman who works almost full time in an engineer's office. "I wasn't around. I never dropped off at preschool; there weren't sports yet. I remember feeling so isolated. You really have to work at it if you're a working mom. When we first moved, I told my husband, 'I hate this town. There's no one like us.' It was all nannies at the playground."

We Need a Community of Moms

Another woman in the group concurred with Kim about the feelings of isolation: "I think it's really hard finding a community of moms who will accept you when you are working. I have a good group now but I found I had to work really hard to get to know them. Two are stay-at-home moms; we have this nice thing—they help me with my daughter and I try to help when I can."

I can personally attest to the benefits of a strong mother network. When I couldn't chaperone a field trip, my friend, who was able to get time off of work and did accompany the class to Plimoth Plantation, sent me pictures of my daughter throughout the day. When I had to work on my son's birthday, his friend's mother had a cupcake and candle waiting for him after school. And weekly I rely on friends to drive my daughter to and from a dance class that starts before my workday ends. When a working woman doesn't have those connections, she worries about what her children are missing. I feel it in my gut when Hillary, a fashion stylist in Manhattan, says, "The plight of every working woman is to be there for the children."

"A few years back, my daughter wanted to go to swim team," says Selena, a risk manager at an investment bank with two kids, aged eight and twelve, and a husband who works at a hospital. "I couldn't find anybody to take her to swim team. She was crying. At that time she was in kindergarten. I felt so sad that I couldn't do things other mothers can do. Now she knows. She will say, 'It's okay.' My two children are very special. I am so proud of them. It's tough."

Should I Stay or Go?

Selena says she can relate to the movie *I Don't Know How She Does It*, about a mother of two working in financial services. "My industry is not very women friendly. This type of job requires a long time commitment. If I really want to be more successful, I need to pull more hours. Before this job I was senior manager. I managed thirty people—very highly educated people—fifteen PhDs, fifteen people offshore. I had to be in the office by seven and leave after seven. I kind of enjoyed the job. It was interesting and I enjoyed the people I worked with. But I lost that job in 2008. If I really want to, I can go back to managing twenty people; the schedule will be tough. My son is in seventh grade. If I have to go back to that kind of lifestyle, I won't have much time with my kids. I will feel more satisfied in my career but I'm going to sacrifice my kids. I keep debating, should I go back? Should I stay here? For me, it's a difficult call."

False Choices

Selena's choices don't feel like choices at all. If she chooses career, her children may suffer. If she scales back, her family's financial security could take a hit; she tells me her husband used to change jobs frequently. And if she chooses to scale back at work or turn down a new assignment, does she freeze her earning potential or perhaps become a target in the event of a downsizing? Never mind her personal satisfaction; that is pushed to the bottom of her priority list.

Selena's story illustrates how the statistics and the common narrative about working women don't tell the full story. It's not that women don't want to work. It's not that women aren't willing to work. It's that women see too few viable options to accomplish what they need. They need to contribute to or provide for their family's financial security. And in order to do that, they need to stay on track at work—if not the fast track, then at least the middle of the road in our current up-or-out corporate culture. At the same time, they, along with their spouse or partner if they have one, need to be the steward of their family's well-being.

Kicking the Can

Our current culture is structured so that work and family priorities compete against each other, and therefore women are making false choices every day. I met a woman who has had a very successful career at a major brokerage house, and she's worried about what's next: "I've gotten good at my job. But with a family, I struggle. Do I really need to do that next challenge? So I keep kicking the can. I look at people who do it. Do they work that much harder than me? A new job, a new role... I'm going to have to do it really well. Should I stay easy? Do you max out if you're also balancing a family?"

Anne McCabe Triana, who cofounded a financial planning and wealth management firm after eleven years in financial services, confirms the pressures, especially in her industry. "I know the Wall Street culture. It's true that if you leave earlier people talk about you behind your back. Productivity is not valued. Hours are valued." She says the focus is on being successful at work while everything else is "down the tubes."

Renee Moadel is a physician working in nuclear medicine and a mother who is divorced and remarried. Her husband is an engineer who has his own firm. Renee is clear that family comes first and, as a result, she thinks her career has suffered. "My work is flexible enough that I can plan it so I can be 100 percent with my son. He's fourteen now. From the time he was born, I was all over it; it was such a joy. I don't really travel for work. I avoid it. That may limit my career to some degree. I could give talks and get more accolades; I'm not sure it would translate into a raise."

The Dreaded Mommy Track

The threat of the mommy track is real. Women know that if they make decisions that favor family, they risk damaging their chances for career advancement and better compensation, even if they are pulling their weight at work. Likewise, if they make decisions that favor their career, they, and their families, can suffer. As a result, some women place themselves on the mommy track while others try to steer clear of it.

One woman, who was in sales and now works part time, says she gave up her career because the commute from Long Island to Manhattan took too much time away from her family. And even though her current employer allows her to make her own hours as long as she completes her work, she's not interested in advancing because she doesn't want to take her focus away from her family. "I know I'll never aspire to be too much higher up. I'm middle management and I'm not going to get too far because of everything else. You sometimes take the cards life dealt you."

Stephanie is a client service associate for a wealth management company. She and her husband have two kids, a ten-year-old boy and a six-year-old girl. "I always dreamt of being the mom who does everything, but you can't be mom and career woman who does everything. Most of my company…one parent stays home. I work in an office of twenty-five people—five have families. My boss made me feel really bad that he thought I wasn't pulling my weight. How much earlier can I possibly get here? Definitely being in the office is important. It's okay to take an occasional child sick day, but you can't be the one doing car-pool run. I like having a career but I don't want to go to business functions at night. I like having time with my kids."

Ten O'Clock E-Mails

And it's not just men who are scrutinizing moms at work. Lee, a new mom and owner of her own company, is very sensitive to the way she and another mother are perceived in the office. Lee gets to work at 9:30, even though her staff is at their desks by 9:00. Before the baby, she worked out in the morning and never gave her arrival time a second thought; it was her privilege as the owner to arrive when she wanted to. Now she spends her mornings with her daughter and worries that may send the wrong message. "At our office, there's only one other parent. She has some flexibility but it's become a challenge. She leaves every day at four to pick up at day care. There are better ways to manage it." Lee worries that her team of mostly twenty-somethings will think that only mothers get flexible options and resent them for it.

Another woman asks Lee: "But how does the corporate culture change unless you bring that work–life culture around?" Ten of us have gathered to discuss work–life flexibility.

"For me, I feel better about myself and this other mom if we're sending e-mails at ten at night," admits Lee.

When a business owner who is herself a new mother admits that she wants to see working mothers logging on after the baby goes to bed at night in order to demonstrate commitment to career, you can see that the challenges of today's women aren't that different from those Sally dealt with in the 1980s. Women need to manage the mom factor at work, which often means overcompensating in order to prove "the kid" isn't affecting the career.

Managing Maternity Leave

Another woman, an IT director, actively managed her time out of the office when she was having a baby. "I networked through my pregnancy and I emphasized my husband's great schedule. I had this fear they were going to write me off. It's so weird. No guy would be at a job saying, 'Well, my wife's at home.' They're sizing you up—how old are you? When will you have babies? Are you married? They don't want to invest in you.

"Technology helps me. I really like what I do, so I answered e-mails on maternity leave. I told my boss I'd check e-mail once every twenty-four hours. It made me feel better. My fear was I'd be so disconnected. I tried to stay connected, within reason, so I could walk back in and have credibility, especially with the third child."

Is Flextime a Trap?

Beware the false hope of flextime, the women I spoke with cautioned. "Flextime is a total joke," the IT director says. "They cut your pay. Work from home? Cut your pay. If you have a doctor's appointment, fine. But if I asked for a day from home formally every week, that's a bigger deal. There have been women who've done it and they say don't even do it. They will cut your pay."

But other women point out that flextime is a viable option for men at work—and perhaps that's because they frame it differently. Says Stephanie, who's sweating what time she gets to work, "No one faces the fact that one of the guys goes out to eat every day for an hour and a half."

"A lot of the men coach," says Linda the commercial banker. "They leave early to do that. What's the difference? But that's considered cool."

Good Dads, Distracted Moms

A successful managing director at a Wall Street investment firm tells me she gets more flex requests from the men on her team than from the women. "They have no trouble telling me Suzy's gonna blow the clarinet. In fact, they're proud of that.

I grew up in the days when you didn't ever expose you needed to take time off for kids. That's the other side of it—when they elect to be the good dad, they're good guys."

Women face that double standard every day: mothers who take time for their children are viewed as less committed while fathers who do the same are "good guys." Some women decide the benefits outweigh the risks and do want to take advantage of work–life policies, but they can hit roadblocks. When I was pregnant and looking for advice on managing my career post-baby, I read articles about companies with private nursing rooms and women who job shared. But talks with my HR department only yielded reams of paperwork and no answers. I was convinced these wonderful, mother-friendly policies were just folklore. My suspicions were further cemented when I ended up in that spider-infested electrical closet pumping breast milk after my son was born and then in a coed bathroom after my daughter was born.

Negotiating Invisible Benefits

Shana spoke about finding solutions for working mothers: "The amount of proactivity it takes is really a lot. And it's coming at a time when, for me, I'm just coming out of this chronic exhaustion. And I negotiate something that doesn't exist. These alternative arrangements are elusive. Even if you're in a marriage where people are going to split things down the middle, I don't know anyone who can continue at work as they have. For each individual to have to guess that in advance, when you could have the business world tackle this problem…"

She's right. The business world should be tackling this problem. Kate, Meghan, Kelly, Selena—these women want to work. They want to contribute, be productive, and excel. It's just that the way they do that may not look the same as the methods of the guy in the next office. Shana, Renee, and Stephanie are all willing to do their fair share. None of them is asking to be rewarded and compensated for a job she didn't do. They're asking for job opportunities to be there even if they don't tackle them in the same way their male counterparts do.

As I write this, there is a blizzard, a perfect storm, according to meteorologists, outside my window. My father and my husband think the best strategy for snow removal is to shovel a little bit several times throughout the storm. I prefer to wait to shovel until after the snow has stopped falling and get it all done at once. In fact, I find doing it all at once works better with my other time commitments—my kids want me to play board games and take them sledding when we have snowstorms, and my boss expects me to stay productive on e-mail and the company VPN. My approach looks different from the men's, but the result will be the same—the stairs and driveway will be cleared of snow.

Just as I approach snow removal differently from the men in my life, women may take a different approach to managing work and life. When businesses listen to the women who work for them and actively seek alternative solutions to work–life challenges, they will find better ways to weather any storm.

But first, women need to clean up the mess at home.

LESSONS FROM THE LADIES

WOMEN:

- Ask for help. Don't try to do it all alone. Ask your partner, spouse, friends, and family.
- Breadwinners and stay-at-home mothers can make powerful allies. Form friendships and partnerships with the women in your community.

EMPLOYERS:

- Women want meaningful work with fewer hours. Part-time shouldn't mean less valuable.
- Don't assume pregnant workers aren't coming back to work. Check your assumptions and don't perpetuate stereotypes.
- Change the up-or-out culture. Companies benefit from great value and talent at all levels.
- Face time and productivity are not the same thing. Let workers harness technology to manage their work and their lives.

3

The Mess at Home:
America Has a Housework Gap

When I first meet Sharon, the analyst at an investment firm with two children, ages eight and five, she tells me she and her husband split family and home responsibilities fifty-fifty. That seems fair. They both work full time, and in fact Sharon significantly outearns her husband. But she quickly amends that statement. "It's complicated, but it's probably sixty-forty."

Sharon says that while she does most of the indoor chores and he does most of the outdoor work, many of his assignments are task-oriented and take place once a week, whereas her assignments—laundry and child care, for example, are constant.

"Cars are totally on him. He stays on top of the oil tank and water tank. He's much more into technology; he will spend a lot of time trying to get the computer to play on the TV. I couldn't care less. He would like a new outlet. I couldn't care less. Of course, he would probably schedule the electrician to come the day I'm home." Sharon works from home on Tuesdays, and her home life usually bleeds into her workday. She describes her work-from-home days as, "proactively running performance data and packing snacks."

One of her husband's project-oriented tasks is the lawn. "He gets absolved of other duties because he's doing yard work. As a point of pride, he wants to do it. I would rather pay for someone to come on Wednesday and get him back on the weekend." I hear this same refrain from a number of women. Their husbands go out to mow the lawn on Saturday, with a football game on their headsets, and are tied up for hours while the wives run errands, clean the house, and entertain the children.

Cleaning for the Cleaners

Outsourcing, however, isn't a magic pill. Most of the women I interviewed who could afford to hire help with the housework did so. But that doesn't mean it's not a source of conflict in their marriages. After all, someone has to do the pre-cleaning cleaning. "We used to fight over the prep for the cleaning lady," said one woman. "He would throw his hands up and say, 'It's ridiculous you clean up for the housecleaner.'"

"We have that conversation at least once a month," said another woman, who works in health-care marketing. "And by conversation I mean screaming. And by screaming I mean me." Her neighbor complained jokingly that she never gets to appreciate the clean house, because her husband gets home before she does on cleaning day. "I don't get a chance to see it clean." She says she comes home and the place is already trashed. "I say to him, 'I don't understand how this happened.' He's like, 'You're crazy,' and I'm like, 'No, you're delusional.' Sometimes I'm not sure the cleaner is worth it."

Sharon, who does have a housekeeper but needs to maintain order in between appointments, is critical of her husband's homemaking. "He buys the groceries and is responsible for all cooking; we eat out twice a week as a result. When he does the shopping, he stops at Starbucks, drives around a little bit. Me? I have a list and it's all about efficiency. He doesn't put his clothes away—it's like a three-foot pile of laundry. And he doesn't value shutting cabinets." Regardless of her feelings, the couple doesn't fight about it.

"I accept it to a large degree," says Sharon. "I think it's just they don't have an awareness. My husband was raised in a very feminist household but he just doesn't see it. His brain doesn't work in those ways. There's a reason men don't wake up when a baby cries or walk past a laundry basket that needs to go upstairs. They don't see things the way we do. They don't see that pile of mail. But my husband looks at the roof and I never look at the roof."

The Havoc of Half Days

The school system is a much bigger source of stress for Sharon than sharing housework with her husband is. The public schools in her town close at 12:30 every Tuesday and six additional Thursdays throughout the year. She has her daughter in an afterschool program on Tuesdays, but the program requires Sharon to also pay for Thursdays, even though she doesn't use it that day. On Thursdays, her daughter goes to Hebrew school and Sharon relies on another family to drive her there. To reciprocate, she tries to have the other family's daughter over for playdates as much as she can. She worries about what would happen if she could no longer rely on her neighbors for transportation. "I'm hoping we keep the relationship going for the next ten years with that family. That's the kind of stress my family isn't thinking about."

"Don't Be a Bitch"

"My husband and I had a big fight at the start of the school year," Sharon tells me. "I noticed the Thursday day off in February was scheduled for a Wednesday, so I sent an e-mail to the PTO office and said, 'I'm curious why it's a Wednesday.'" Sharon didn't hear back and she pushed the issue in December but her husband cautioned her, "Don't be a bitch."

"Pointing out that something is inefficient gets that label," she says. "But it's disorganized not to communicate. Maybe there's a good reason; it's probably rippling from something else that I need to know about. So tell me, because I haven't stopped thinking about it since July. And I'm concerned I'm going to be the one who's affected. Thankfully, I've been with my company seven years and have established some flexibility."

I feel her pain. Sharon and I, although we live in different towns, commiserated over the fact that we both received notices that our children's art would be on display in district-wide art exhibits the night before the events. Neither one of us made it to our respective shows, as we both had prior work commitments. And yet both of us have enough seniority and personal equity at work that we could have rearranged our schedules if we had advance notice. "[The planning] doesn't happen overnight. So why give us one day of notice?" Sharon asks.

Good question. At my child's show, hundreds of little masterpieces lined the halls. It must have taken time to hang all of that art, probably more than a day. The high school band was performing. I assume they were given more than twenty-four hours' notice. Refreshments were served. That required planning.

Interestingly, neither Sharon nor I received much sympathy when we complained about our situations, even thought it's a scenario played out across the country. "I've gotten a day's notice that my child is going to get an award," one woman tells me. "Stop with the middle-of-the-day thing. My eight-year-old is asking, 'Can you do it this year? Can you chaperone?' I mean, I book vacations four months out."

Why Can't You Come, Mommy?

The general consensus is that working mothers should accept the fact that they are going to miss out on school events. But that doesn't have to be the case all the time. We accept that there are many things we cannot do because we are working. But we can't reconcile a child's broken heart when the situation could have been avoided with planning and communication. When I told my son I couldn't attend his show, I could tell he was trying to be mature, saying to me, "That's okay." But it wasn't okay. If you've ever watched a child on a school stage scan the audience anxiously looking for parents and then waving and smiling when they are spotted, you understand how important family involvement is to a child.

Another working woman tells me her daughter is constantly asking her to come into her classroom: 'Why can't you come in, Mommy?' she asks. When I finally came in for secret reader she was thrilled. If I could just live that day over and over I would." Working mothers don't expect it to be easy, but we're never going to accept when our children are negatively impacted and the situation could have been avoided.

All parents, especially working mothers, have to consciously manage perceptions at work. If we are serious about our careers we need to be seen as dedicated to the job. Yes, it has become more acceptable to work from home on the day of a school event or hold a conference call while driving to meet the bus, but it's a fine line. We are constantly seeking the right balance of work and family.

True, no one will lie on her deathbed and wish she had picked the meeting over the school play, but many will lie awake in their own beds at night wondering how to make more money in order to help pay for their child's education.

When a working mother picks and chooses which school events she will attend, she is also thinking about any contingency days she may need for sick days and snow days too. She is constantly weighing the risk/rewards for every decision she makes to be at work or at home. Where is the greater payoff—the client call or the teacher conference? What carries a higher penalty—miss the meeting or miss the field trip?

My Lists Have Sub-Lists

"It's exhausting," says Sharon, about trying to stay on top of her family's schedule. "You're always thinking ahead to the next thing. I make lists in my sleep and my lists have sub-lists. My calendar is my life."

By the time Sharon and I are done talking, she's decided she and her husband have an eighty–twenty split of family-related chores. "I am basically 100 percent responsible for winter gear and the replacement of all winter gear, as it inevitably gets lost; bathing suits, towels, goggles, and water shoes in the summer—more daily laundry; all kids' clothing shopping—what sizes they wear, what needs to be purchased, weeding out/donating old clothing; my kids' birthday parties, including planning, booking, inviting, goody bags, food purchasing/ordering, thank-you notes—any and all thank-you notes, for that matter; all RSVPs; most gift giving; paying the bills; all packing for trips for the kids—including overnight camp for my daughter—a huge job; arranging the cleaning people; cleaning for the cleaning people; all kid haircuts; trash and recycling; making the grocery list; homework; bathing the kids. And thus I live with a near-constant eyelid twitch."

The Invisible Task List

Sharon's list is full of the invisible tasks, the tasks that don't necessarily show up on a chore list but still require time and mental energy. These tasks, with a few exceptions, over-whelmingly fall to women, no matter what a couple's work–life arrangement is.

Take Tania, a high-powered, successful managing director at a Wall Street investment firm and the sole breadwinner for her family. She and her husband have four kids and made the decision fifteen or twenty years ago that he would stay home because her career was taking off. "In the '90s I was having kids and traveling to Europe all the time. Even after that I was alternating weeks between California and New York. You can't outsource at that level unless you're going to hire some kind of governess out of an English novel."

Tania makes no qualms about what she thinks is a fair division of responsibilities between herself and her husband. "When dinner's not on the table I'm pissed. It's not that there isn't dinner; it's, 'Can you figure out what time I get home? Why do I have to tell you I'm on the bus—'cause a woman would know.' You work all day, come home, pace for twenty minutes debating whether or not to shove cereal in your mouth cause you're starving and you haven't eaten since one and now it's eight."

As far as cleaning goes, Tania doesn't think it's her job. "I'm kind of a bitch. I'm Robert Young from *Father Knows Best*. If I were Laura Petrie, would Dick come home and clean the house?" she asks, referencing the popular 1960s sitcom *The Dick Van Dyke Show*. Men, as a rule, are not expected to come home from work and take care of the home. But the same isn't true for women.

Stay-at-Home Dads Aren't Moms

When things break down in Tania's family life, she thinks part of the problem can be attributed to her husband defining the role of stay-at-home spouse differently than many women do. "The men see what quote, unquote, stay-at-home-mothers do, and only see the physical. They don't plan anything. They don't check calendars to see if something is viable. They think the job description is menial. It's like the difference between a house manager and a house maintainer. My husband seems to think that managing the house and the kids, that these are elective. So he enters into projects that he's interested in. Like, my son is seventeen—my husband got a twenty-five-year-old Mercedes and rebuilt it for my son. He'll totally clear his schedule to accommodate that because his home role is elected. Imagine if you were home and your husband came home from work after being in the city for hours and hours and you said, 'I ordered Chinese takeout because I was making a quilt all day.' The roles of stay-at-home women and men are not interchangeable. I don't even know if the guys know what the job description is."

Don't Blame Biology

Don't try to tell Tania that biology makes men and women view the roles of stay-at-home spouse differently. "I don't believe in that stuff...," Tania says. "I have never had a biological urge to clean anything."

Tania says that, with her husband, small but important things fall through the cracks. "The other thing I find, at least with my husband, is they don't remember all the detail stuff. They don't even remember what grade the kids are in. The school will call the house and he'll let it go to voice mail and tell me to call the school back. Or they just haven't checked that box on their little opt-in box. I have said to my husband numerous times, 'Just put it in your Blackberry, set yourself an alarm.' I've had my husband forget to take my daughter to her tennis lessons—I mean, that kind of stuff." As a result, the invisible tasks fall to Tania.

"If your kids have an issue, you can read it," Tania asserts. "There are all these different emotional intelligence things going on. They fly over the guy's head. They just don't get it. They just don't. My daughter has a chronic medical condition that kind of comes and goes. I can tell in two seconds if something is off. Meanwhile, he could take her to a tennis lesson with a fever."

We Need You at Work

The issue with invisible tasks isn't just one of an equitable marriage. It's the mental energy these tasks consume and the impact that has on a woman at work. Stephanie, the customer service associate whose boss said she wasn't pulling her weight, says she assumed responsibility for most of the invisible tasks until people in her office noticed. "When we first had kids I was like, 'Yup, that's me.' The week sign-up happens at camp, it consumes me. I don't want to disappoint my kid. I spend fifteen minutes every day making sure everything doesn't fall through the crack. But I decided it was jeopardizing my career. My boss called me aside and said, 'I know you're juggling, but we need you.'"

As a result of that discussion, Stephanie tries to hide these responsibilities from her coworkers. "Thank God babysitters have text and e-mail. I try for school not to call me. I use technology a lot. I use texting. It just makes it so much easier."

JJ DiGeronimo, a director at a large technology company, says the invisible tasks are exhausting: "Although I'm very organized, there are few moments that I can just kick back and relax without worrying about all the things I have yet to check off my list. It's fueled some of the controversy in our house, since my husband does a better job of unplugging even if it is for just a few minutes. It's likely not going to change for you, for me, or for any woman that is juggling too many commitments. I think women are tremendous; they're just tremendous, but many women I meet are committed to too many things and they are exhausted."

One solution is to pull men into these tasks. If women keep the invisible tasks hidden from their spouses, how can we expect them to help? Lisa Gates, cofounder of She Negotiates, a training program for women, thinks so: "The thinking part is such a burden. I think we do our mates a disservice by not involving them. There was a particular time four or five years ago—we were in a hard economic time—there was a strike in my husband's industry. And the thinking wore me out. It was almost an obsession. I was creating graphs in my head and I realized I do not have enough support. I am not leaning on my friends. I didn't even consider my husband part of the process. I didn't trust the answers he would come up with."

Are You a Maternal Gatekeeper?

Gates raises an interesting point. Women are shouldering the majority of responsibilities at home, but how much of their burden is self-imposed? Jen Deaderick, a writer from Cambridge, Massachusetts, cautions that women need to be aware of trapping themselves in the homemaker role: "One of the things I noticed other women doing is they would decide things have to be a certain way; the husband doesn't know how to do it right. They would trap themselves. Which can be rather intoxicating."

Melissa Williams, an assistant professor of business at Emory University, says the behavior Jen references is a form of maternal gatekeeping. Maternal gatekeepers, through criticism or nonverbalized rules, can limit or inhibit their spouses' participation in household chores and child care.

Williams and UC Berkeley psychologist Serena Chen conducted a study that indicated women who run their households have fewer career ambitions and less interest in promotions and raises at work. Through a series of experiments, they found that ambition wasn't affected when women shared household responsibilities with their spouses, only when they controlled them. While both female and male survey participants agreed that having control of household decisions is desirable and advantageous, only women indicated that actually having that control impacted their career ambitions.

Williams says it's not that women are less interested in power than men are, but that women often feel like their two domains—work and home—are zero-sum. "Men can pursue both simultaneously," she says.

Her coauthor, Chen, says, "To realize true gender equality in both the private and public spheres, our results suggest that women may need to at least partially abdicate their role of ultimate household deciders, and men must agree to share such decision making."

Men Aren't Mind Readers

Abdicating some responsibilities in the home takes training and discipline. Kelly, the attorney, says one thing women should do is ask their spouses for the help they want; it's good for both managing the chores and the relationship. "I kind of think men get a bad rap with women, but they're not mind readers and I don't see any problem if I have to ask for [what I need]. I don't have a problem saying, 'Can you do this for me or can you make sure the trash gets taken out?' I think it makes for a better marriage. Plus, I'm a divorce attorney," she says, implying she'd rather ask for what she needs than become a client.

One reason more women may not ask, however, is that they find it easier to do things themselves. That may be a good short-term solution, but it doesn't help in the longer run. We need to work toward sustainable options that work over the course of our careers and our marriages. "I know about things like doing laundry or tending to the house, hanging pictures and things," says Jen. "All that kind of stuff I just know. And it becomes so much work to kind of instruct your husband. That's another trap—it's easier to do myself. He does dishes and laundry and trash. He's not very good at it but I don't want to do it. It's always a struggle."

That struggle may involve lowering our standards and accepting that a task that isn't completed to our standards is still a task completed. It also involves letting ourselves off the hook for results that are short of perfection. As Lisa, a development officer for a nonprofit, says, "It's about quality of output." Lisa says she'd be likely to send her kids to school on a cold, snowy day with hat, mittens, snow pants for recess, and a healthy snack, and her husband might send them to school missing one of those items. Either way, the child would most likely be fine. Another woman agrees: yes, the children will be fine, but she says women judge themselves harshly. "If my husband brings them to school and they say, 'Dad, you forgot my snack.' He thinks, 'I forgot the snack.' But if I forget the snack, I think, 'I'm a bad mom.'"

Getting to a place of acceptance often involves getting out of the way. "If I'm away it's fine, but my husband and I do things so differently that if I come home and he's in the middle…" says the woman who works in the engineer's office. "It's easier for me to be out of town or literally stop somewhere and read a book. I don't want to come home in the middle of it. I just basically need to relax but it just gets you so wound up."

Her friends support the hands-off strategy; not only does it give a mother more freedom, it also allows a husband to be his own parent, not his wife's version of a parent. "[My husband] does much, much better when I'm not there because he defaults to 'Linda will do it,'" says the commercial banker. "But when I'm gone he'll take the kids and do more things with them because I'm not there to backfill. It's actually good for him, and the kids enjoy it. It's a different dynamic. And he steps up and does a great job. And I get home, and the house is standing, and we still have two kids, and the cat is in the house. He will rise to the occasion."

The Kids Are Alive

Linda's neighbor, a scientific director for a pharmaceutical company, concurs that women need to get out of the house sometimes and let men manage on their own. She says, "The kids are alive, you have your own relationship with them, you figure out what works. Don't involve me as long as they wear something that covers their genitalia."

Suggesting women step out of the way and let their husbands step up may sound like victim blaming. It's not. The interpretation should not be that it is women's behavior that leads to the fact that they do a disproportionate amount of housework and child care. But in some cases, it is at least part of the problem and therefore is one strategy women can deploy to attempt to shift the balance of responsibilities. Whether women give in to their spouse's approach to parenting, stay out of the house and read a book until the chores are done, or ask their husbands to do things their way, women who want to let go of some responsibilities need to make an active decision to do so. We receive so many external messages about what a good mother should do—serve well-balanced meals three times a day, maintain a picture-perfect home, and turn out children who resemble J. Crew models—that we need to consciously reprogram our way of thinking about what good parenting looks like.

Sondra, a business owner who's been married twenty-five years and has three grown children, took on both the housework and the invisible tasks because she wanted her children to have a certain type of childhood: "Throughout their childhood and our young lives, my husband and I attempted to craft a semi-balanced share of child rearing and housework, using some outside help. However, in the end I led and took care of finances, cooking, shopping, family activities, holidays, birthdays, schoolwork, sports, discipline, day-to-day housework, and family plans. Mostly because he just didn't see it needing attention. I think we are more attuned, as women, to the finer details of life, the organization and the project management needed to keep a family and home going. He was happy to sit back, oversee, and lend judgment. It was much more challenging when the kids were young. I started working when my daughter went to kindergarten."

Sondra continues, "The kids were really central to me carrying the load. I wanted them to have a certain lifestyle. And if my husband wasn't going to lead that, the alternative of not having that happen was unacceptable for me. So we're kind of stuck in this paradox where we want our worldview to happen but we want someone else to make it happen. My kids now say, 'We had the best childhood—the things we did, the camps we had.' So I know I did the right thing."

I Lost Respect for Him

For Sondra, carrying the load at home didn't just impact her career, it impacted her marriage. "What's happened since the kids left…My husband and I have lost a lot in the relationship. I don't have a lot of respect for him. I never felt like he…boy, this is hard to say…really lived up to his role. And it's not that he didn't know what I expected. It wasn't a big hide-and-seek game for me. I was clear. But, really, the relationship…we don't have a relationship, primarily because I know I have a lot of anger. It definitely clouds the way my husband and I relate now. We're trying to make it work and I do see him, as he gets older too, maturing into a different type of partner.

"As a fifty-year-old woman whose children are gone, there are a lot of scars there and a lot of things getting in my way and it always seems to take him by surprise. My husband is very compassionate, very loving. Our relationship is based on need and not necessarily love. This is a difficult observation too—I sometimes think had my husband faced more adversity if I hadn't pretty much taken care of everything, if I had maybe stepped back and forced him to take care of different things, he might not be unemployed. I guess in some ways I was an obstacle to that. It's hard to say. I don't regret anything in life. I certainly don't regret staying home with my kids. I love my life. I love my career. I love my kids. And, essentially, I love my husband. Would I want him to be a different person? But what would I be giving up?

"I noticed when I was young the stress we had was mostly about things. Who's going to feed the baby? Who's going to unload the dishwasher? As we got older it became more about substance. My daughter was diagnosed with anorexia and the arguments were about who…and I do have to say he really stepped up during that time. He tried to take the lead as much as possible. It was an effort for me but I allowed him to. There's a trust issue if you haven't been able to trust him to do stuff around the house but now trust him with your daughter's illness. I still know I carried the burden for 90 percent. But there were parts of allowing him to step up."

Of course, the inequity in household chores found in so many American households, the resulting schisms in many relationships, and the negative impact that often occurs for women in the workplace won't be solved by a simple platitude like, "Lower your standards, ladies." But it is something in our power to address. And then we need to tackle many other factors, including societal pressures, media influences, and, dare we say it, sexism.

It's Not Sexism; It's a Weird Given

Dr. Dawn DeLavallade is a virtual radiologist who works from home interpreting CT scans, ultrasounds, and X-rays from hospitals across the country. She works seven nights in a row, followed by seven nights off. The schedule gives her the flexibility she needs to be available to her son while her husband travels building his own business. Dawn says she would love more help at home from her husband, who she says works long hours in a demanding job. "My husband sometimes feels like he doesn't have to do anything," she says. "I cut back. I took a voluntary pay cut to make time for my son. A part of that is self-inflicted—if you teach someone they can always count on you, that's what they do. And when he's home he wants to put his feet up. Even if I say I fixed dinner and it's your turn to clean, it's still not done the next morning. A part of it is, it's still kind of a king-of-the-castle feeling there—he just feels like he doesn't have to do it."

Maria from the engineering office wants more help too. "I argue with my husband every summer. He can never, ever get home for what I need, but on golf Wednesday, come hell or high water, at ten past four he leaves to golf. He goes with the guys he works with, not even with clients. Are you kidding me?

The rest of the family suffers all week because he works until nine every other night. I'll say, 'Can you pick up the kids?' 'No, no, no, I have a job.'"

King of the castle. Putting his feet up. Golf before family. It sounds like old-fashioned, 1950s sexism doesn't it? But most women aren't willing to call it that, although they usually can point out friends with sexist husbands.

"My husband is great," says Leslie, who left graduate school when she got pregnant with her son. "He doesn't even need me to say, 'Hey, can you vacuum?' There are a few things he needs to be pushed to do. If there are dirty dishes in the sink or clean dishes in the dishwasher...I do have friends whose husbands work their butts off and they come home and put a beer and the clicker in their hands and they don't get up until they go to bed."

Monika works from home full time. Her husband works in corporate communications. They have two children, ages five and three. "I do probably 90 percent of the household chores," she tells me. "My husband's primary responsibility is making lunches. We decided at one point he'd do meal planning and groceries. He does it about 5 percent of the time. I've tried not doing [housework], and that just drives me more crazy. I would like to think that I'm not nagging about things that don't need to get done. But the boys need lunch. People need to eat dinner. Every once in a while the house needs to get cleaned. We had a cleaning lady but it's not in the finances. It's a hard struggle—do I take the weekend to clean the house or spend time as a family? Usually we choose family. But since I work from home, I'm the one who has to live in that."

"My husband is perfectly willing to step in," Monika continues. "I don't think he considers any of it to be my job. He doesn't notice it and isn't as good at remembering and planning ahead for things. He just doesn't see it. It's very frustrating. He's so good at his job and he's a really good friend and dad. We've never been a couple to fight about money, it's just the division of labor."

"Yesterday I was home to do child care," says Ilana Garber, a rabbi and mother of two who is married to a musician. "While I'm the breadwinner, not primary, it was sort of just a given that I would cancel my appointments and...and it's not sexism, it's just sort of this weird given." This given Ilana describes is a common theme in many marriages. Even among couples who defy traditional gender roles with regard to breadwinning, child-care responsibilities are often just assumed to be a woman's concern.

Making a Quantum Leap

"Sexism is the easy answer," says Lisa, a mother of two who works 80 percent full time and is married to an architect. "But I think that answer feels a little unsatisfying," she says. "I think I do much more than my husband. But he feels like he does so much more than he ever thought he'd do. The leap we are asking [men] to take is a quantum leap. I think it's changing at a lightning speed but I don't think it changes instantly."

Describing what's taking place in women's homes and workplaces as sexism may feel unsatisfactory, but unless we name the problem, it's difficult to change it. If therapists can't even tackle the issue, as we saw with the woman whose marriage counselor told her she had to quit her job, who can address this "weird given?" Part of the solution lies in our ability to shift our thinking about housework and child care as they relate to work from women's issues to parenting issues. Women's roles have evolved over the years to include breadwinning. Now we should expect men's roles to shift as well and include more family and household responsibilities.

"What struck me when we first had kids and he was changing jobs, he never asked about flextime and all the questions that any mom with two kids under three would ask," says Lisa. "As I've gotten back from the edge of exhaustion and rage that I typically felt when the kids were little...I think the workplace for men has to be understood and changed as much as it has to change for women. So many men are still worried about taking time off, and many don't take the paid leave they are entitled to. When they don't take their leave, it puts the women who do take it at a disadvantage—they are gone for weeks or months in a way that men aren't."

Lisa, rightly so, suggests another part of the solution for the inequities women face at work and at home is for men to demand and take the same parental benefits women do. Still, she acknowledges, it's not a simple fix. "Looking back I can see that the forces my husband was fighting were very powerful. At his Christmas party there was a guy with a baby in a Baby Bjorn. Everyone was like, 'That's so sweet.' That guy was gone a few months later. And the problem…what does the workplace do? It doesn't surprise me that women don't choose the bigger job. Someone needs a flexible job."

Husbands Aren't Bad People

Michelle Parrinello-Cason, a PhD student and full-time faculty member at a community college, agrees with Lisa on two fronts. The first is that most husbands aren't overt sexists; their behavior is more ingrained and maybe even subconscious. The second is that motherhood exposes an inevitable chasm in marriages that skews in the man's favor. "At least, speaking for me and for my friends, I don't think our husbands are bad people, they just don't even realize that this is happening," says Michelle. She is married to an attorney and they have one child. "I'm just at home more; more of my forty hours are spent in my house. It was something my husband and I had to work through." And like Lisa, Michelle experienced pregnancy as a defining work–life moment. "I was breastfeeding. I was the one who went through the physical stress of pregnancy. When I would talk to my husband, he was like, 'Okay, I get it.' But it was so frustrating to negotiate. I was so overwhelmed to even tell him. And all the questions we got were, 'What are you going to do?' He was sitting right there; he's going to do things too."

I remember fielding similar questions when I was pregnant. Up until that point, I enjoyed what I felt was a fairly progressive partnership with my husband. I was the primary breadwinner. I kept my name. I felt like "I am woman, hear me roar." But when I got pregnant, I was the one who felt like I needed a nap at my desk. I was the one who had to miss hours of work to go to doctor's appointments. I was the one whose stomach entered the conference room seconds before the rest of my body did. And colleagues and clients commented I was cute, or huge, or, worse, they touched my stomach. My husband was about to become a parent too, but his work identity hadn't shifted, while mine had morphed from smart, hard-working employee to woman-about-to-take-leave. I hated the whole experience and felt blindsided by the changes. When my friend innocently offered to take me to Babies "R" Us to help me register for nursery items, I exploded at her and wanted to know why the hell she didn't ask my husband to go buy baby things?

I Don't Do Diapers

Some of the working women I spoke with have learned how to address the issue of becoming a mother with more grace and skill than I exhibited in snapping at my friend. Ilana refuses to change diapers. "Unless my husband is not in the house, I will not change a diaper. It stems from the early few weeks. The baby would wake up and I had to get ready to nurse. I was in charge of input and he was in charge of output. It's a wonderful thing he does a lot of that stuff."

And even though men, like women, may suffer some back-lash at work when they exercise their right to parental benefits, one C-level executive I spoke with and her husband have had a positive experience treating the work–life issue as a family issue rather than as a mother issue. "One thing that has helped tremendously, after I took three months of maternity leave, is my husband took one month," says the marketing executive for a health-care nonprofit. "I would recommend it to anyone. What happened was, when I was on maternity leave, I was in this state where I was constantly checking in, 'When are you going to be home?' Everything was lovely, but I wanted to hand over the baby, and if you haven't been there, you can't relate. He'd say, 'I'll be home at five,' and I'd be watching the clock, thinking, 'I can make it.' But when he got home, he'd spend an hour unloading tools. I told him, 'We need to have a conversation about being home or being on the property and being home able to take the child.' In the fourth month, he was calling me at work asking when I'd be home and I loved it. Now he just gets the rhythm—what it means to be with the kid all day every day, what it means to be home all day."

The workplace needs to recognize raising children is a parenting issue, not a mom issue. Our spouses need to know it's a parenting issue, and the schools need to know it too. "The schools default to moms. The schools absolutely default to moms," says Tania, the sole breadwinner, echoing a complaint I heard from so many women.

The commercial banker tells me, "I get notices about PTO meetings at 8:45 Monday morning. Okay, who doesn't have a staff meeting Mondays? Who's available for that? Or, the e-mail comes out on Wednesday to pick up your stuff for the fund-raiser for two o'clock on Thursday. Two o'clock on Thursday? How am I going to do that? So I e-mailed the PTO president and asked if she had any suggestions for working parents. She delivered them, which I thought was really nice but also overkill—like I kind of felt like, 'Well, shouldn't I be able to pick up?' "

Co-Parenting Is Possible

Krissa, a full-time, self-employed consultant, says she and her husband, who is also self-employed, completely co-run their home. She said it took a few years to get to that place and that part of it involved educating her children's schools. "We pushed to have his name added to everything. No conversation happens without both of us. All the teachers know we have to both be included on everything." One small but significant change that happened in her school district was the classroom directory, which used to only list contact information for children's mothers, now includes a place to list the fathers too.

Michelle, the PhD student, has also retrained her children's school to stop deferring to her on everything. "When my daughter has a fever or something, they immediately call me. And I'll say it's my husband's turn to get her."

For women like Michelle, changing the status quo is more than an issue of equity. It's about raising the next generation to be that much more aware than this one. Her husband shares grocery shopping duties and she wonders if her daughter notices. "I just hope that I can make her enough of a feminist so that she makes her own decision." Michelle has a healthy, long-term approach to her current situation. While we work to find balance in our own lives, we also need to prepare the next generation for changing gender roles and dynamics at work and at home.

Is Babysitting a Trap?

Alison, a writer, also wants to raise her four daughters to be self-sufficient and self-fulfilled. She says that when her girls were small, "I wanted my daughters to think of nobody else in the world but themselves, to follow their own goals, to just bypass all that nurturing and babysitting shit, and get jobs that pay good money. And all of that stuff, it's a struggle. I think a lot of it is internally programmed."

"I was successful," Alison says. "Very few [of my daughters] babysat. I think it's the first step in the trap, I really think it is. It's that sort of mommy's little helper thing. If she wants to make cookies, she's in charge. She's going to be on a stepstool measuring things. She's not going to be opening the fridge to get me an egg. She's not going to be helping me. She's going to be the boss."

Alison and Michelle know that women can't be what they don't see. And what so many women see are images of women as supermom, not superwoman.

Of course, no woman is really a superwoman—at least I'm not. Still you don't need to remind me. Here are six things I hope you never say to me or any working mother:

Do you have to work? First of all, that's none of your business. Second of all, it's completely irrelevant. Some women enjoy working. But if you mean, do I have to work from two to two thirty on Wednesday when the class is decorating gingerbread houses? Yes, I have a meeting with my boss at that time. Otherwise, I'd try to rearrange my schedule...again.

Don't feel guilty. Who said anything about guilt? You did, not me. I may be frustrated that the teacher didn't choose the field trip chaperones until three days before the outing and that's not enough notice for me to miss work. I may be crazed because I am trying to find a skin-colored leotard with black straps by tomorrow. Maybe I feel disappointed that I am going to miss my daughter's play because I'll be out of town. Most likely, I am exhausted because I got up at 5:00 a.m. to get some work done before the science fair. But I don't feel guilty about providing a paycheck for my family.

This is important, so do your best to be there. I don't need to be reminded how important it is for me to be involved in my child's education. In fact, I think it's the administration or school staff or PTO board that needs the reminder if they're the ones responsible for planning an event at an inconvenient time or with too little notice. I do my best every day. But I cannot reschedule a client meeting or business trip or deadline with little notice. If I could, I would.

Don't worry. Your child will be fine if you're not there. Who said anything about my child? I know my child will survive if I don't volunteer at the holiday bazaar. And I even think my child benefits from my missing a concert or two. What better way to learn to perform for the joy of it instead of for the applause? But I understand that life is short and our children grow up fast, and so I want to be there.

I don't know how you do it. I couldn't stand to miss out on my child's activities. I don't need to explain why you should never say this. It's horrible and you know it.

I guess if you're going to work, you have to accept that you'll miss out. As a working parent, I don't expect to be at every event. But what I do expect is enough planning, communication, and courtesy that I can choose the events I will miss and the events I will use my vacation or personal time to attend. What I will never accept is missing events that I may have been able to attend if only I had enough notice.

And the one thing we'd love to hear you say?

You're right. All parents are busy and need more notice and flexibility. Let's work together to effect positive change.

LESSONS FROM THE LADIES

WOMEN:

- Outsource housework if you can afford to.
- Don't keep the invisible tasks invisible from your partner/spouse. Ask for help.
- Do keep invisible tasks invisible at work. Use texting and personal e-mail accounts as much as possible to get things done.
- Avoid maternal gatekeeping. Your way is not the only way.

SCHOOL STAFF:

- Plan and communicate. Working parents need advance notice to attend school events.
- Don't default to mom. Understand the roles of parents and who to contact when.

SPOUSES:

- Help out with housework; discuss an equitable plan and stick to it.
- Take paternity leave if it is available to you.
- Take advantage of leave and flex benefits as appropriate.

4

Mom and the Media:
The Influences That Shape Us

Because my husband and I are comfortable breaking traditional gender roles with regard to family and work (except for the fact that he's a lousy housekeeper and I think I have to handle too many invisible tasks), I wanted to understand why so many working women were still hampered by housework and child care, why they couldn't break free of that role in order to focus more on career. But as I started to talk to more and more women, I realized the answer was obvious and the question was irrelevant. It's what we do about it that matters.

Avital Norman Nathman, a freelance writer and mother to one, believes stereotypical gender roles are ingrained in our minds. "I think a lot of it is society and societal expectations. It's going to take more than ten, twenty, thirty years to provide an alternative of what a family should look like, what a breadwinner should look like."

Of course it is. How many of us were raised in traditional homes, where Dad worked and Mom took care of the kids and the home? And how many of us whose parents are still alive see our parents living out the same roles today, even though Dad retired years ago? If Dad's not out at work all day anymore, then why is Mom still waiting on him? And who's planning family holidays and buying gifts for the grandkids? Most likely it's not Papa. "My parents had a very traditional marriage," one female primary breadwinner tells me. "And now I feel that pressure of home, hearth, and kids."

And even women who come from different backgrounds are affected. Meghan, whose husband opened an auto body shop after losing his job, says, "I think, too, it's stressful because [my husband] wants to provide. His mom worked all the time. She was a single mother. She did sometimes two or three jobs to make ends meet. Even with that, though, he still has this mentality that the women should be home."

Lynn works part time, is married to a commercial real estate broker, has two teenage children, and describes herself as an ex-feminist. Her decision to not pursue a full-time job was influenced by her working mother. "My mom wasn't around when I was growing up," Lynn tells me. "My mom was the only working mom I knew. I like that I've been to every one of my daughter's cheerleading games. My mother always said, 'I had to work.' 'No, no. You didn't have to work. You chose a lifestyle. To say you had to work is a cop-out.' I often talk to my friends who are working moms and they are racked with guilt. They get…I don't want to use the word bitter, but there's definitely a form of resentment that comes. I think if you can do it without regret it doesn't matter what you do. My mom was racked with guilt and I can play that guilt card anytime."

Michelle's childhood inspired her to want to work. The PhD student says, "What I saw my mother go through I didn't want to go through. [My father] was an abusive man. But my mother was incredibly paralyzed by an anxiety disorder and agoraphobia. She did 100 percent of the house and child care. She had to clear buying shoes. It was really pretty abusive and restrictive. They divorced when I was twelve. She had married him when she was eighteen. She had been out of the workforce for years. Suddenly she had three kids to support and Dad refused to pay child support until the court ordered he pay some. She was completely on her own. I had to help with the bills when I was fifteen. I remember thinking very clearly, this is never going to happen to me."

We Are Not Our Mothers

We cannot underestimate how much what we see and hear growing up influences the decisions we make as adults. At some point during my childhood I dropped my plans for Unicorn Enterprises and decided to study writing in college. My father told me writing was a hobby, not a career, and so I went off to corporate America in pursuit of that "good job." As clearly as I remember his advice, I remember my mother volunteering in my classroom, walking me home from school, playing dodge-ball with my sisters and me in the driveway after dinner, and drinking tea at our kitchen table with the other mothers in the neighborhood. Those are the images I recall when I think of a mother—a woman who is always present and part of a child's day-to-day routine, a woman whose life revolves around the kitchen and neighborhood. As the sole breadwinner who hops on the commuter rail at 8:17 every morning and returns home at seven o'clock every night, that is not the mother I can be. Still, some weekends I notice I've exhausted myself trying.

"The thing that is hardest for me," says Elizabeth Amorose, the owner of a branding firm and primary breadwinner for her family, "is that my parents are very traditional and raised me to be a housewife. I have this very successful business and my parents in some ways think that I'm a failure. Sometimes I'll call my mom on the way home from work. It's eight o'clock...my parents are white collar, very Catholic. I didn't even know my dad as a kid because he worked all the time. And I think that because I saw my parents have these two very strict gender roles...even though I do expect my husband to do most housework, I will make an effort to give my husband a break now that the shoe is on the other foot. I was raised to be the housewife and he wasn't. My husband had a similar upbringing—very traditional. I have a lifetime of how you take care of the house, so I have to manage him sometimes, which is not good for either of us."

Alison, the writer with four daughters, dropped out of college freshman year because her father wouldn't cosign her loan for tuition. "I only found out later that he didn't think girls should go to college," she says. She met a cadet at West Point and got married. "One of my brothers had gone and my mother made such a big deal of, 'They're such nice kids. They're all achievers, blah, blah, blah.' So I guess when I was that young I figured, well, if I ended up with one of these guys I'd be doing okay." Alison went back to school and finished her degree after she had children and while she was working both on staff at a magazine and as a freelancer for a newspaper. She and her husband recently divorced, and she worries about what advice to give her daughters. "I am very concerned about the whole princess concept, you know. 'Oh, this is it. I'm in love. I don't need anybody else for the rest of my life.' Stupid."

Fairy Tales Aren't Real

Liora Farkovitz knows fairy tales aren't real. She is divorced and remarried, and she and her husband are both working while building a business together. "Louis has a lot of very traditional ideas about a wife and I use very traditional roles to express my love," Liora says, "I like cooking things he likes, and the fact that he really enjoys what I cook feels great. But, when I get really busy he might go a week with deli takeout and deliveries, and he always gets very unhappy about it. He doesn't necessarily say anything, but I can tell there's an internal sulk. While he was ensconced in the breadwinner role and I was at home most of the time, he expected me to take the laundry to the cleaners, fix dinner, run errands, etc., but this was never spoken. It was fine until I started having more demands on my time and noticing that there's a list inside their heads of things we 'should' do and they feel entitled to our roles. The truth is, he believes I should cook, even though he truly sees himself as the modern man. Meanwhile it was dawning on me, 'Just because I have boobs and a vagina you think I should cook!' Doing it because I love him and doing it because I should are two different things! We both have these ideas about what we should or shouldn't have and when our ideas fail to realize— that's when you get into the complexity. Women have a sense of entitlement about a man too—he should earn a paycheck or fix the toilet, and definitely catch any renegade mice. It just depends on where we're from, what our norms are."

I'm Your Coworker, Not Your Wife

If our ideas about gender roles affect how we judge ourselves, we have to expect it will affect our relationships not only with our spouses, but also with the men we work with. Research out of the University of North Carolina, New York University, and the University of Utah suggests that married male employees who have stay-at-home wives are "more likely to exhibit attitudes, beliefs, and behaviors that are harmful to women in the workplace" than men in more modern marriages where the wife works.

In their paper "Marriage Structure and the Gender Revolution in the Workplace," researchers Sreedhari D. Desai, Dolly Chugh, and Arthur Brief illustrate how the men with wives at home "undermine the role of women in the workplace" and tend to view women's presence in the workplace unfavorably, view organizations with female leaders as unattractive, and "deny, more frequently, qualified female employees opportunities for promotion." This research speaks to the need for changes to be made at both the personal and the institutional level. Because even if we've bucked our childhood images of what a good woman and mother is, even if we've sorted out who's doing the laundry and the cooking at home, freeing us to focus on our careers, and even if we have our spouses on board with our desires or need to work and find some semblance of balance and sanity, we can still face subtle and ingrained biases at work from men whose ideals of women are clouding their professional judgment.

I've seen these biases surface in my own professional experiences over and over. I was startled when a client, sitting next to me on a plane, asked me, "Does your husband mind that you're taking this trip with me?" I was twenty-six at the time and didn't know what my husband had to do with the meetings I had worked so hard to arrange in New York. I spent the next five hours of the flight wondering, was my client hitting on me? Was he judging me? Or was he merely expressing some kind of fatherly concern about a young woman traveling across country? I wasn't interested in him thinking any of those things; I only wanted him to be impressed with my work.

In another incident, I stood stunned and slightly embarrassed after a male coworker pulled a pocketknife away from me in front of our coworkers when we were dismantling an exhibit booth after a trade show. "Women shouldn't use knives. They could cut themselves," he said. And I smiled with glee when he proceeded to slice his finger.

And a few years ago I was furious when a client, over lunch at the very expensive hotel where he was staying on business, told me he could no longer pay me for my marketing services but wanted to know whether I would continue to work for him for free. Right before our meeting, he had introduced me to his attorney from a very prestigious firm and joked about the lawyer's hourly fees in the $500 an hour range. In exchange for my services, my client said he could offer me, a professional with twenty years in the industry, "exposure." I politely declined his offer, but to this day I wish I had told him what was going through my mind: I run a business. I feed my family from that business. Exposure doesn't pay for groceries or the mortgage. I am not a recent college grad just starting out and trying to build a portfolio. I am not a housewife with a hobby. I am a breadwinner. And would you ever, ever ask your male attorney to work for exposure?

We Are Making Progress

Despite the very real biases working women face both at home and at work, we should acknowledge and find encouragement in the fact that women are making progress. We may be pumping breast milk in less than ideal conditions, but we do have the opportunity to return to work after having a child. My aunt, just one generation before me, told me she and her coworkers were fired from jobs at the phone company when they announced their pregnancies. Realizing the women who raised us worked in such different cultural climates than we do should spur us to work for even more advancements for ourselves and the next generation.

"I have this great oral history," says Jen Deaderick. "My grandparents had been married for fifty years and my grandmother was complaining that my grandfather didn't do dishes. Years later he started doing the dishes. It took fifty years for him to really get she was upset about it. So clearly they were talking about this in the '70s."

While we should never become complacent about the obstacles and discrimination we may face, and no one wants to wait fifty years for some help in the kitchen, some patience and perspective can help to keep us motivated so we can focus on how we can model new behaviors for ourselves and the generations that will follow us.

"My parents are not even that old and they're so outdated," says Elizabeth. "They were raising me to be a housewife when a lot of my friends weren't. My brothers were forced to study finance in college. They were raised to be businessmen. My sister is a very successful career person. Her husband takes care of their kid. Neither of my brothers ended up being driven businesspeople, yet my sister and I are, even though we were the ones who were essentially raised to be housewives. Kids have to be raised different so everybody can do the house stuff."

It can be done. "I grew up in a very traditional home," says Jan Risher, who works in corporate communications. "If there wasn't a remote control, [my mother] would get up and change the channel for my father. I changed the model from my parents' generation to mine." And Avital grew up in what she describes as a gender-neutral house, and today she and her pharmacist husband split household and child-care responsibilities fairly. "I grew up watching [my father] vacuum and clean and do dishes. And my mom was out in the yard too."

Is Staying Home Antifeminist?

Still, when Avital had a baby, she says, "I felt the pull to stay home. It sounds so antifeminist. But I kind of had it in back of my mind. I'll only have this one child; this is going to be my chance." Wanting to stay home with your child may feel antifeminist to Avital, but it's hardly countercultural.

Women are conflicted. Through our friends, neighbors, family members, coworkers, and the media, we see so many different images of women going to work, staying home, working part time, opting out, leaning in, climbing the ladder, and jumping off, and we're trying to figure out where we fit in. It's why some women still tread carefully in their role as breadwinner.

Hope, a director at an investment firm, works long hours and is the primary breadwinner for her family. Still, she finds herself having to tone down her role outside the office. "Sometimes I feel like I have to thank [my husband], like 'Thank you so much for doing this at home and that at home and that at home.' No one is ever thanking me for going to Phoenix and being gone for five days and getting home and going to the supermarket because there's no food in the house. But I do feel like, you know, it would be nice if you thanked me every once in a while. And it's not...like I said, we are very much in love with one another, but it's almost like going back in time."

Tania, the managing director on Wall Street, despite her clear expectations about responsibilities, finds she too sometimes treads carefully at home. "As a woman, you can't get on [your husband]—maybe it's going to crush their masculinity or whatever. You can't say, 'What do you mean you didn't put my clothes away?' So the woman holds back because you don't want to damage their ego. Men don't care."

She says the holding back also extends to the way some women describe their stay-at-home spouses. "Everybody's husband who stays home, we run a front for. He's a 'day trader' or an 'investment advisor.' He's not running the PTO. But, oh, okay, your husband's a managing director and he makes plenty of money so you stay home. Nobody would question it for a minute."

Tania says it's worth it to play along. "I also think the women who have the stay-at-home guy, they're protecting him because, one, they need this arrangement to have the job they have. And so they protect his status. The women with the stay-at-home husbands are still so much better off than the person who's coming home and trying to frantically microwave burritos. They're shutting up because this isn't optimal but it's more optimal than the alternative. Now I've got a better deal than the other people. The best deal in town would be a real wife."

I Can Talk Kids

Outside our own homes, breadwinners are often conscious about blending in. Hope recounts a party she attended when she first moved into her neighborhood. She said she asked the women what they did but none of them worked. "And I'm like,

'Well, I work, and I do this, and my kids are at the preschool,' and they're like, 'Oh, you should go talk to my husband about that.' I can talk kids; just 'cause I work, I can talk kids. And then they're pissed that I'm talking to their husbands."

Some women feel the pressures of what Tania refers to as the Michaels Mafia, a reference to the arts and crafts store chain Michaels. She talks about women who have "These psychotic roles at school. They devise these craft roles that are completely ridiculous and unnecessary that cause me to jump through hoops." She recalls looking for googly eyes in the aisles of Michaels at night after work. "Or they have a Thanksgiving feast the day before Thanksgiving in a middle-class community."

"The schools do the same thing," Tania says. "They set up activities in the middle of the day and then you send your husband and they treat your husband like he's a freak."

It's interesting, in talking to women about their careers and families I, refreshingly, didn't hear a lot of guilt about women working and being away from their children as a result, but I did hear guilt referenced several times in relation to not helping at school. However, I don't believe guilt is really the right word to convey what these women are feeling. I think discomfort in saying no while other women say yes is more accurate. "Regarding the PTO," says one woman, "I write a check. I get e-mails about 'Come stand at the craft table or go to Michaels to buy stuff.' So now I feel really bad. I don't want to take a day off. But if I don't take a personal day will they think I'm a jerk?" Women, perhaps because so many of us are raised to be helpful and accommodating, don't want to miss work, but don't want to let down the volunteers either.

You Can Say No, You Know

Alison says women have to find a way to accept not being the chair of everything and not being the overachiever. "For so many years I was spreading myself too thin, and as much as I enjoyed spending time with my kids, my priorities were skewed and it became way too much work and not being home enough when they needed me."

Sheila, a regional president for a development company and mother of two, says, "There are so many women who feel like they have to be on the PTO. They have to be on this committee. They have to go on every field trip. You can't do it. You just can't do it all. And the kids, ultimately, they're going to be okay."

Sheila's husband is chair of a nonprofit organization, and his board of directors is made up of four men and nine women. "The women are completely overcommitted. They get on [the board] because they say yes but they are so overcommitted they can't get anything done. So they meet for all this time but it's not really getting done as quickly as it should be," says Sheila.

A friend of mine, another working mother, only participates on her own terms. "I spend so much of my life in meetings, and for a lot of folks PTO is very social," she says. "And I can appreciate that but that's not why I'm going to be involved. Give me a task and I'll run with it and get it done and you'll be psyched with the quality, but let's talk for two hours and no one leaves with any to-dos? It makes me frickin' nuts."

My personal strategy is to organize a raffle every September for my children's elementary school. I let everyone know that is all I am willing to take on for the year. It's the first PTO fundraiser of the year, and it's something I can manage without any help and on my own schedule. By the beginning of October, I've raised a significant amount of money and I am done for another year. I still have to say no throughout the year as different volunteer opportunities arise. But I'm comfortable with my response because I know I've done what I could do and so I don't worry about what others might think I should do.

You Don't Need Goody Bags?

Sybil, who works full time for a major mutual fund company, is married to an attorney and has two sons. She simply says no to unnecessary tasks. "I've loosened up. I don't do goody bags at birthday parties. I don't do Christmas cards, no birth announcements. Unless [my husband] is going to take the lead, I'm not doing it."

The research consultant says thinking in terms of "yes and" is helpful for her when she assesses the additional activities she is willing to take on. If she wants to volunteer, she says, "Yes, I could do that and this is what I need to be successful."

Pinterest Makes Me Feel Bad

In order for women to get comfortable knowing what they really want to take on outside of work and family, and to say no to the things they don't want to do, they need to stop comparing themselves to other women. That's always been difficult to do when the media is constantly bombarding us on television shows, in movies, and in magazines with images of beautiful, well-dressed superwomen who appear to cruise through life with ease and grace. It's become even harder with the proliferation of social media. At least with mainstream media, women can tell themselves that the celebrity women they admire and the lifestyles they covet are carefully crafted and well staffed. But with social media, we see our friends, family, and acquaintances lives up close and personal—or at least we think we do—and we wonder why can't we have what they have.

A random peak at Facebook tells me one former colleague's business is booming, another's husband surprised her with tickets to a concert, yet another threw an elaborate, pirate-themed birthday party for her son, an old college friend has purchased an oceanfront summer home, and my cousin took her family to Puerto Rico on vacation. I, on the other hand, didn't get home from work in time to see my kids, my husband is upstairs snoring, and I am sitting alone working in my very messy living room wearing pajamas purchased at a discount store.

Monika says, "Things like Pinterest and Facebook and seeing what the stay-at-homes I'm friends with do, like planning these elaborate parties for their kids and celebrating these special moments, that I just can't get it together to do for my kids...There's that struggle of seeing all of that and thinking, 'How do they make it work?' "

Avital Norman Nathman says, "In an age of social media, where people put forth a Photoshopped ideal of their lives on Facebook, Pinterest, and mommy blogs, it perpetuates this myth." The myth, of course, is that of the good mother, the ideal woman who lives a perfect life with a perfect family in a perfect home. We have to tell ourselves that these images don't reflect everyday life. And more importantly, we have to tell each other the same thing.

A survey of four hundred women conducted by daily deal company Eversave in 2011 revealed that 85 percent of women report feeling annoyed by their online friends, with 32 percent annoyed by their friends' bragging about their "seemingly perfect lives" and 40 percent describing a friend as a "poser" who projects a picture-perfect life online. But while we know on one level that most people share only the best moments on sites like Facebook and Instagram and that the images they curate on Pinterest aren't necessarily reflective of their actual homes, craft skills, or wardrobes, we still can't help but feel the way Sharon feels when she says, "Pinterest make me feel worse about things."

Lifestyle blogs aren't much better. Holly Hilgenberg wrote an article for *Bitch* magazine in which she explained why the proliferation of lifestyle bloggers—women who blog about parenting, decorating, food, and crafts—is so disconcerting. "Forms of media that have glorified and promoted the home front as an exclusively female domain, after all, have never been in short supply, from sitcoms to shelter magazines to store catalogs. But an accumulation of such choices promotes a homogenous narrative indistinguishable from those that have come before."

With former coworkers on Facebook throwing elaborate parties for three-year-olds, feminists who want to be home with their kids, and investment executives thanking their husbands for cleaning, it's easy to be confounded by all of our choices as modern women. On one hand, we have so many choices that we are both lucky and overwhelmed. On the other hand, we ascribe choice to situations where what look like options really aren't—situations where women are forced out of the workplace because of barriers, both overt and subtle, both at work and at home.

Should We All Be Moms-in-Chief?

For every fictional Alicia Florrik of *The Good Wife*, who returns to a successful law career after quitting to be a stay-at-home mother and political wife, with only enough stress to fill a sixty-minute drama, television gives us a Julia Braverman on *Parenthood*, who quits her law career after she misses her daughter's dance recital due to a work crisis. We have as role models both former First Lady, Senator, and Secretary of State Hillary Rodham Clinton, who left public office with more political clout than, arguably, any woman or man in this country, as well as First Lady Michelle Obama, who told us at the 2012 Democratic National Convention, "At the end of the day, my most important title is still mom-in-chief." These two women spin vastly different images of themselves, yet both top the Gallup Poll's list of most admired women in the world.

Both women attended Ivy League schools and practiced law. Both women are mothers to daughters. Both women are politically savvy. But perhaps learning from the flak Clinton received after saying during her husband's presidential campaign, "I suppose I could have stayed home and baked cookies and had teas, but what I decided to do was fulfill my profession," Obama has been presented by the president's political team as more mother than working mother.

Working mothers were a political hot potato in the 2012 political cycle. After Republican presidential nominee Mitt Romney positioned his wife, Ann, as his political advisor on women-related issues, CNN contributor and Democratic strategist Hillary Rosen ignited a firestorm by saying Ann Romney had never worked a day in her life. Ann Romney responded on Twitter, saying, "I made a choice to stay home and raise five boys. Believe me, it was hard work." The First Lady defended Romney with her own tweet, which read, "Every mother works hard, and every woman deserves to be respected." The commentary almost sparked a full-out mommy war that even the president himself weighed in on when he said, "There's no tougher job than being a mom."

Given the sensitivities around the way women are perceived and the ways the media pits those of us who work outside the home against those of us who do not, it makes sense for Michelle Obama to remind us she's mom-in-chief first. But what message does it send? Following the First Lady's convention appearance, Lisa Belkin wrote about Michelle Obama on *The Huffington Post*, "Here we have...A woman whose political instincts...clearly tell her that her bona fides, her palatability, is still tied to being seen as mom and wife. I am not disappointed because I think she is wrong. I am worried because I fear she is right."

A Zero-Sum Game

Is it any wonder women often feel like their two domains—work and home—are zero-sum, when that's the message we receive from our political leaders, the media, and even our peers? This false dichotomy creates feelings of confusion and ambiguity. And it's one of the reasons women need to talk to each other about the challenges they face and the choices they make. Because it's among the women in our everyday lives that we will find everyday solutions to managing work and home.

When Marissa Mayer was named CEO of Yahoo! women celebrated. There are so few women running Fortune 500 companies, let alone technology companies, that we saw her appointment as progress. Plus, she was pregnant. But then the thirty-seven-year-old CEO announced she would take a very abbreviated maternity leave, and the reactions were mixed. Avital felt that Mayer missed an opportunity to make it easier for other women who want to take leave. "You might not want to take leave but there are plenty of women who do," she said in reference to Mayer. "There is a responsibility of women in positions of power and also for men. We can't say jobs are only important."

Marissa Mayer Let Me Down

Julie, a public relations executive with two children, said, "Marissa Mayer was a huge disappointment to me. I was really frustrated with that. Our generation is just not willing to sacrifice family for work." But for every woman who felt betrayed by Mayer there was a woman who celebrated her right to choose what worked best for her and her child.

Media reviews were mixed too. Jessica Grose wrote at *Bloomberg Businessweek*, "Perhaps Mayer's choice has created such controversy because it makes the rest of us so painfully aware that we're stuck without options at all." Katherine Reynolds Lewis wrote at *Fortune*, "Her decision seems emblematic of a workaholic culture that leaves too little time for family or even personal health, preventing either men or women from 'having it all.' Could Mayer be setting unrealistic expectations for young women hoping to follow in her footsteps?"

The commentary I found most unsettling, from a *Forbes* article, was this passage: "We already know from Hewlett-Packard's Meg Whitman, Facebook's Sheryl Sandberg, and a handful of other C-level executive moms that women can indeed combine motherhood with a rise to the top ranks of corporate America." The year was 2012 and we were confirming that mothers could be CEOs. Can you imagine making that statement about fathers?

LESSONS FROM THE LADIES

WOMEN:

- Be aware of the outside influences that affect the way you view working and parenting.
- Stay focused on the long-term view. Women have made tremendous progress in the workplace, and we still have much to do.
- Do not succumb to the Michaels Mafia. We all have our own unique roles to fill.
- Learn to say no. You don't have to do it all.
- Practice "yes and" thinking for mutually satisfying outcomes.
- Don't compare yourself with other women. It's a no-win scenario.

EMPLOYERS:

- Notice how personal beliefs are showing up in the workplace.
- Face time and productivity are not the same thing. Let workers embrace technology to manage their work and their lives.

5

What About the Men:
Why We Need to Talk About
Parenting, Not Mothering

Why, in 2012, seventy years after Rosie the Riveter emerged as a symbol of women's power and value in the workplace, is a major American business magazine confirming that mothers can indeed be CEOs? Shouldn't we already know that? We should, but we're not all convinced. And part of the problem is the common sentiment, reinforced by our president, that being a mother is the hardest job. That is not true.

Mothering Is Not the Hardest Job

After the Ann Romney and Hillary Rosen dispute about working mothers during the last presidential election, I wrote a blog post in which I said, mothering is not the hardest job, parenting is. If we are ever going to get past the gender gap in this country both at home and at work, we need to shift our thinking about mothering to include parenting. Some may find this statement ironic in a book focused on working women, but the fact is, there are issues unique to women that we need to address—their levels of participation in the workforce, the gender-based obstacles they face at work and at home, societal expectations of women and mothers in particular—and there are the issues we need to address for all parents and workers, regardless of gender. And if we work together on these issues, won't all of us eventually win?

Take the discussion about mothers choosing to work or to stay home. It is usually toxic and fraught with emotional land mines. The mere hint of the discussion can spark a "mommy war," and that is good for nobody. Part of it is a language issue. Personally, I bristle at the term full-time mother. I work outside the home eight, sometimes ten, hours a day. Does that make me a part-time mother? I don't see it that way.

And then there is the term working mother, a label I am given because I have a job in an office. Does that mean that a woman who stays home and manages her household and family doesn't work? I don't think she'd see it that way. But to be perfectly honest, when I hear a mother who doesn't earn a paycheck explain to me her reasons for staying home, the benefits her family derives from her decision, and the many tasks she accomplishes as a result, I bristle. Because what does that imply about me? And if I explain that my children aren't shortchanged, that we get all those things accomplished in my household too, then am I implying that the woman who stays home is inefficient or exaggerating? It's a no-win conversation. And we aren't having those discussions about men. There are no daddy wars, because we aren't scrutinizing men's career choices, nor are we grading their parenting. And why should we? There is no one-size-fits-all approach to being a man or a woman, a father or a mother.

Stay-at-Home Fathers Emerge

Yes, we're starting to see the term stay-at-home father crop up. Labels are valuable for measuring, and it's interesting to note that, according to the latest data from the U.S. Census Bureau, the number of stay-at-home fathers in the United States has more than doubled in the past ten years, with the current number at 154,000. But for the most part, men with children are merely referred to as fathers or dads. How often do you hear the term working father in reference to a coworker or a neighbor? Not very often. We know Marissa Mayer, the current CEO of Yahoo!, is a mother. Did we ever discuss or wonder if Scott Thompson, the former CEO, was a father? He is, by the way, to three kids.

Why do we separate mothering from parenting when we talk about work? I earn a paycheck; my husband does not. Some days I have it tougher than he does. I get up at five in the morning just to carve out time for myself—to exercise or to write. My husband sleeps until six thirty because he can exercise or read while the kids are in school. If I'm having a bad day, I still have to sit upright at my desk and keep my head in the game. He has between the hours of nine and three to be in a bad mood in private if he needs it. And some days, he has it tougher, and I walk out the door thinking, "Good luck, buddy," as he deals with whining, tears, missing homework, shirts that don't feel right, playground politics, and a packed schedule that goes until eight o'clock at night.

But for the things that really matter, we are both there. When the kids are sad or hurt or sick, when we are worried about their health, their futures, their emotional well-being, we're both there. That's the hardest job—parenting—and we both own it.

We should apply the same common-sense approach to fair pay, paid sick leave, parental leave, affordable child care, flexibility, and even reproductive rights. These are not just women's issues, although the media labels them as such. Heck, they're not even just parents' issues. These are issues that impact every worker, regardless of gender or parenting status, although parents stand to lose a lot when they don't exist.

The Wage Gap: Not a Woman's Issue

Let's look at the wage gap as an example of the way so-called women's issues affect both genders. As we've stated, the median earnings of women who worked full time, year-round were 77 percent of that for men working full time, year-round. And mothers suffer a per-child wage penalty of approximately 5 percent, on average. Considering that more than half of American women who work are breadwinners contributing at least some part of the necessary income to maintain their households, and that there are twenty-three million mothers on the national payroll, the gap is quite disconcerting.

Women's earning may be reduced, but the items they're paying for are not. If we're relying on their salaries to cover health care, child care, and housing costs, consumer goods like clothing and groceries, and savings for retirement, then the wage gap affects women, men, our families, and our country's economic stability. Theses items are not reduced by 23 percent when a woman pays for them. It doesn't take an economist to understand that when American families are struggling, consumer spending goes down. And consumer spending accounts for approximately 70 percent of total economic activity. Closing the gap is more than a woman's issue. It's more than a family issue. It's an economic issue.

Parents Need Paid Sick Leave

Paid sick leave has economic implications too. We've heard the stories of couples playing the "whose job is more important game" when a child is sick and can't go to day care or school. That's a high-class problem for some, because at least those couples have jobs and the option of staying home. Forty-eight percent of workers in the private sector don't receive any paid sick days, and included in that number are more than thirteen million working women. For the sixty-six million Americans providing unpaid care to family and friends, a lack of paid sick leave makes their work–life situations unmanageable.

"It's my busiest week of the year, and I've been talking non-stop about being thoroughly stressed by all the final work products I have due by December 31, except that because day care is closed the last week of December, it all has to be done this week," says Shana, the nonprofit fund-raiser. "The frustration started when my husband realized he had to take a few days off or 'lose' the paid time off before the end of the year . . . but was very pouty that I couldn't manage to take off a few days as well so we could spend time together while the kid is in day care. But here we are, December 18 . . . I've been essentially single parenting since Sunday because my husband is sick. Not only do I have my hands totally full with my curious, feisty, also sort of sniffly, teething nineteen-month-old, but my husband has been whining and asking for me to fetch him extra blankets and tea and make him soup and go to the store to get him the Gatorade he likes and now, of course, I've put off whatever I was doing so I could take him to the doctor, drive him to the pharmacy . . . finally getting to work a little now that he's down for a nap. And needless to say, it's not reciprocal . . . the last time I was sick he went to a five-day conference, leaving me with a fever and a ten-month-old, and I'm actually fighting through one hell of a cough right now. But, you know, I can just talk to my clients and explain."

According to the National Partnership for Women & Families, adults without paid sick days are 1.5 times more likely than adults with paid sick days to go to work when they have a contagious illness. They can skip work and risk losing their jobs or come to work and put their coworkers and customers at risk. The Centers for Disease Control and Prevention predicted that last year's flu season would end up costing businesses $10.5 billion in direct costs for hospitalizations and outpatient visits for adults. That number didn't factor in lost productivity at work. This is not a women's issue. This is not a parents' issue. This is a workplace issue and it affects everyone.

What About Paternity Leave?

Imagine if we stopped talking about maternity leave and started talking about parenting leave? While we won't change the fact that women carry and deliver babies, we could change the dynamic around how we care for them and how we think about parenting in the workplace. In 2012, the U.S. Equal Employment Opportunity Commission received 3,745 pregnancy discrimination complaints. We can only wonder, if more working fathers were asking for and taking paternity leave, or asking for sick time and flex arrangements, would negative attitudes and misperceptions about working mothers shift as a result?

For that to happen, companies have to offer paid leave for men and women. We know the United States is one of only four countries that don't offer paid leave to new mothers. Paternity leave is even scarcer. Under the Family Medical Leave Act, men can take leave, but like women, only if they work in an organization that is covered. Companies with fifty or more employees are typically eligible, and the men requesting leave must work there 1,250 hours during the twelve months prior to the start of leave, at a location where fifty or more employees have worked for the employer for twelve months. According to the Families and Work Institute National Study of Employers (NSE), men on paternity leave are much less likely than women on maternity leave to receive some replacement pay during their leave.

Avital Norman Nathman's husband asked for paternity leave and was met with major resistance by his higher-ups. "How can you talk about having it all when you can't even have the basics?" she asks. "My husband had to fight for his leave. He said, 'I kind of want to be home with my wife and kid.' The expectation is men take two or three days. My husband was like, 'I'm also the parent.'" It will take more men like Avital's husband speaking up and asking for time to remove the stigma for both men and women who parent and work. Women, who we could argue generally have much more precarious job security than men, have had to demand the benefits they need. Now we need men to join the cause in force. They have less risk, potentially, and more to gain, for all of us.

Backup Day Care Reduces Stress

Affordable child care is a parenting issue too. Women may disproportionately shoulder the burden of managing child-care options, but that shouldn't be the case, and with more women serving as breadwinners, they're helping to pay for it too. According to Child Care Aware® of America, whose mission is ensuring access to high-quality, affordable child care, in 2011 the average annual cost of full-time child care for an infant in a center ranged from approximately $4,600 in Mississippi to nearly $15,000 in Massachusetts. The costs for a four-year-old ranged from approximately $3,900 in Mississippi to nearly $11,700 in Massachusetts. That's steep.

And American parents have very few choices for backup child care when their children are sick. According to the NSE, only 6 percent of companies surveyed in 2005 offered backup child care, and that numbered dropped to a mere 3 percent in 2012. "My husband worked for Microsoft and the benefits included backup day care," one woman told me. "It was amazing. I wish more companies offered it. It would cut the stress." Worrying about how to care for your child when you have to work and they are sick should not be a women's issue. That should be a parenting issue.

Families Need Choices

Reproductive rights, although so often framed as a political issue and a religious issue, are also a workplace issue. Parents, and women especially, must have the ability to plan their families if they are going to be able to plan their careers. Currently, we don't live and work in a land where we are free from pregnancy discrimination, have parenting leave for all workers, and are assured of paid sick leave when we need to care for ourselves and our family members. Having a child does impact a woman's career, and therefore her family's life. The women I talked to are constantly weighing their children's emotional needs against their family's financial needs. They're worried about turning down a promotion or a plum assignment, as it might affect their earning potential. They're weighing the pros and cons of being more available when their children are infants or toddlers or teens. Yes, having a baby is unique to a woman. But being a caregiver, both emotional and financial, is gender-blind. Women and men need access to a full spectrum of reproductive health choices and the freedom to decide what is best for themselves and their families with regard to family planning.

Dad's Flexibility Helps Mom

The one topic traditionally considered a woman's issue that has many men joining the conversation is flexible work arrangements. The Families and Work Institute National Study of Employers (NSE), states that "flexibility that enhances an employee's ability to decide when and where they accomplish their work tasks is on the rise with increases in the proportion of employers allowing at least some employees access to flextime and place and choices in managing time since 2005. On the other hand, flexibility around reduced time, caregiving leaves, and flex careers has declined since 2005." And yet the study found that employees who work in flexible work-places are more likely to report higher levels of job satisfaction, less negative and stressful spillover from job to home, better mental health, and lower stress levels. The women I talked to reported that when their husbands had flexibility at work, it made a difference in the women's home and work lives.

Linda, the commercial banker, changed jobs several years ago in an effort to find some work–life balance. "It has completely backfired. Horribly," she says. Linda has not found any more balance in her current position. Her husband works full time as a sales representative for a pharmaceuticals company and has flexibility. "That's how we keep it together," says Linda. If her husband didn't have flexibility, Linda would be struggling even more than she is to manage work and home.

And Laura, an executive director for a nonprofit, said both she and her husband made deliberate career choices in order to have the flexibility they wanted for their family. Their decisions were spurred in part after Laura was unable to negotiate well-compensated flex hours following the birth of their first child. "There were two women before me who had babies, but they both left. For me, it wasn't an option at the time so I took my maternity leave. I got eight weeks unpaid." Laura points out that the organization she worked for at the time had a mission of helping families in need. "And yet they have nothing, nothing at all. I ended up trying to negotiate part time; I was asking to work from home one day a week. I ended up negotiating going back three days a week but I took a huge pay cut. A few years before, my husband was still working a million hours a week as a chef and then we started talking about having kids. We said, 'This isn't realistic.'"

Eventually, Laura's husband made a career change and became a teacher. "As far as his schedule, it's pretty awesome. He's off when the kids are off and he's home in the afternoon. I wouldn't be able to do my job if he didn't have his job because my schedule is so all over the place." Laura says she made it clear with her next employer that flexibility was critical. She told them, "I am going to drop my kids off and I am going to pick them up and I will do nighttime meetings and all that. They get it. And I do drop them off in the morning and I do, most days, pick my daughter up at three. So basically from, like, two forty-five to seven o'clock I'm sort of off duty unless someone really needs me." Laura says she often sneaks in and out of her office to check e-mail, make a quick call, or write a memo while the kids are doing homework. "When I sneak in work when I'm supposed to be on family time, I feel like I'm cheating on my family."

When her husband comes home from work they figure out what they have going on as far as meetings and their children's activities. Laura says, "Yesterday he walked in and I said, 'I'm off duty. No one knock on my office door.' And I went in and I closed it and I worked for a couple of hours. And then it's dinnertime and we do all of [our daughters'] activities. Then I work after they go to bed. So I'm very sleep deprived, but I do it in order to be able to have the flexibility to be there for them and I don't mind it. We chose our careers right now because it works for our family. We both came to the decision that time is worth more to us than money."

Men Want Family Time Too

In the introduction to the *Global Study on Men and Work-Life Integration*, Peter Linkow and Jan Civian of management consulting firm WFD Consulting wrote, "Men still perceive work–life programs as primarily serving the needs of women, and most use work–life options at lower rates than women." Interestingly, but not surprising, the men surveyed for the study, "reported more difficulty finding time to spend with family, and women reported more difficulty finding time for chores and errands." However, Linkow and Civian did note men and women mostly share similar workplace cultural barriers

to managing work and family. They went on to say, "It's time
to lay to rest the notion that these are women's issues only, and
focus on individualizing workplaces to support business objec-
tives and personal goals."

WorldatWork's Alliance for Work-Life Progress, a global
human resources association that cosponsored the study,
gathered approximately two dozen participants, most of them
male, to discuss work–life balance. They determined that the
common idea that men derive their identities from work while
women derive them from family are unfounded and that both
men and women believe they have been punished for using
work–life benefits.

One of the ways men and women can work together to create more flex-friendly environments is to support each other's
desire and decisions to go flex. Yes, we women joke and complain about how men can leave early to golf but not to parent,
or that coaching seems to be an acceptable reason to leave early
but school pickup does not. "If a man leaves early you hear
what a good dad he is," says Julie, the public relations executive. "But if a mom has to leave early for soccer practice…
There are gender biases and it's infuriating." We need to take
the reasons for flex out of the equation and work on how best to
meet our business and personal goals in a more forgiving work
environment rather than judge why our coworkers are calling
into a meeting from home or leaving the office by three.

Having men advocate for fair wages, paid leave, and work-
from-home days is important. So is having men advocate for
women. And to make that happen, we need to invite them into
the discussion.

Gender Biases Remain a Major Barrier

There is a growing body of research that shows women at the
top of organizations are good for the bottom line. There is
also plenty of research that documents both the subtle and

overt barriers women face in the workplace. Men supporting women is good for business, good for families, and good for their own work–life goals.

Men can support women's advancement, and therefore a more gender-balanced corporate and family culture, by being aware of the inherent biases built into performance evaluations, formal and informal networks, and a woman's ability to speak up, negotiate, and self-promote without suffering backlash.

Catalyst, an organization that supports women's advancements at work, released a study several years ago titled *Cascading Gender Biases, Compounding Effects: An Assessment of Talent Management Systems.* The study found that gender biases and stereotypes were "unconsciously embedded" into performance review processes. Because most skills assessments are developed by or with senior management, they typically view the characteristics of that group most favorably. And because senior management in corporate America is still predominantly male, the assessments favor more masculine attributes over stereotypical feminine attributes like collaborating and nurturing. Men in leadership positions can influence the way those assessments and tools are developed and ensure that a broader set of attributes are evaluated.

Catalyst also studied the importance of sponsorship in advancing a career and issued a report titled *Sponsoring Women to Success.* A study of four thousand MBAs showed that men are still more likely than women to have effective sponsors in the workplace. Unlike mentors, who provide practical advice, sponsors typically lend their personal and professional capital to advancing another's career. The report noted, "Lack of sponsorship is one indicator of what's really been holding many women back—exclusion from organizations' most influential networks." With so few women at the top of organizations, women seek male sponsors to help them advance and build strong networks.

I'm Lonely at Work

Holli, a lawyer, has seen many of her female colleagues drop out of the workforce, and she believes their absence could impact her career. "Where does that leave those of us who have to stay in the game, or want to? It's a pretty isolated place. I have fewer contacts to network with and fewer close friends who are truly in the same situation." She talks about the importance of building a book of business in order for attorneys to earn equity partnerships. "What's so important is the business generation. It's a numbers game in the sense that women leaving the field results in fewer close professional contacts for their female colleagues, which is likely to result in fewer referral sources over the long term. I have very few law school friends who are still practicing law—and I think that is a problem."

Holli found some women-focused networking events and groups to be ineffectual because a surprising number of the women who attended were not fully engaged in the workplace. Some were looking to reenter the workforce or to change career paths, and the women who attended for these reasons were unlikely to be decision makers. "The problems of women leaving the workplace...yes, it leaves the families in an economically vulnerable position. And, collectively, it's really problematic for those of us who have to keep working, who are surviving and hopefully thriving with fewer and fewer women around.

"It seems to me that many women experience a sense of isolation in the workplace that may lead them to bow out if they are economically able to do so. On some level, they think to themselves, 'The next tier up is all guys. So why do I think I would make it there?' Or what about the phenomenon of seeing the pack of men going to lunch? If there are no women for you to go to lunch with, being at work becomes less satisfying."

I understand what she means. I once worked as the vice president of Marketing for a family-owned business run by three brothers. I was the only female vice president. The head of Sales and I, in order to foster a strong relationship between our two departments, shared an office. At least twice a week, one of the owners would stop by and ask my office mate, a male, to go to lunch. I was never invited. The only women in the company were administrative staff, part-time consultants, and the women who reported to me on my team. I was very lonely at work and knew I was missing out on the informal bonding and decision making that took place over a lunch table instead of a conference table. It was a frustrating and lonely experience.

"Who wants to get up and go to work, only to be snubbed?" asks Holli. "You can't force your way in. You can't make people have lunch with you. And it seems to me that a woman who feels isolated in this way is more likely to leave the workforce if she can."

Holli notes, however, that lunch should be a good way to build a sense of camaraderie with men—and is probably preferable to other activities. "Lunch is a pretty safe environment. Most of the time you probably won't be turned down if you ask someone to lunch. But a lot of the other socializing happens on the golf course and at nighttime events, where it is often just not comfortable for women to participate with men."

I can understand that too. When I first started as the head of Marketing, and before my officemate was hired, I was attending a trade show with the all-male sales team. I thought it would be a good idea to go out for drinks with them when the show ended to start to build informal relationships. The group proceeded to get drunk. One of the men we were with was hitting on young women, and my group was egging him on, encouraging him to "score." I left early, embarrassed and angry. I knew if I stayed I would either have to act like one of the guys and pretend their behavior and comments didn't bother me or call them out and risk having them alienate me at work. After that night, I rarely went out socially at work, even though I traveled with the sales team frequently.

Holli says there are things companies can do to help women network more easily: "A workplace can encourage group events; buy four or six tickets instead of two." Regarding the possibility of simply networking with men in response to a diminishing list of female contacts, Holli says it can be a difficult task: "What that really means is going out to networking events or professional activities, meeting a bunch of forty- to fifty-year-old guys, developing relationships with these men that rise to a level where they trust you, view you as competent, and view you as a professional, and doing all of this at night, during nonworking hours. And, by the way, your prospective contacts and business sources are all married and have families of their own, and may have their own discomfort with socializing across gender lines in certain settings. This is a very tall order. There is no doubt in my mind that it is far easier for women to develop close and meaningful professional relationships with other women. But, if there are fewer women in the workplace with whom to develop those relationships, you have to find a way to compensate—and it is not easy."

Women, for their part, can make the first moves as well as look outside their own organizations. Perhaps I could have found a place at that lunch table years ago if I had asked the owner and the head of Sales to lunch. And now, even though I work with plenty of female peers, I try to have lunch at least twice a month with a woman outside my own organization and even my own industry. Our day to day jobs may be different but usually our experiences, challenges, ideas, and even contacts, are all relevant to each other.

There's a Brain Drain Happening

"Pregnancy didn't impact my career," Holli says. "I'm much more focused on what the next twenty-five years of work look like—having a happy and successful career. I would like to see more women stay in it. But it's not my place to tell another woman to do so. There are women out there working who would like to see more women working. Life in the work-place would be more satisfying. I believe there is a horrible brain drain happening in numerous professions based on the attrition rate for well-educated, talented women. Still, I would never presume to tell another woman what she should do in her own situation."

The women who do stay in the game, those who want to rise to the top of an organization, need to carefully manage how they advocate for themselves through both negotiation and self-promotion. It's been documented that women fear backlash from advocating for themselves, and this can impact whether they ask for raises, favorable assignments, or promotions. The fear stems from a double bind, which Catalyst documents in its report *The Double-Bind Dilemma for Women in Leadership: Damned If You Do, Doomed If You Don't*. The report points out, "When women act in ways that are consistent with gender stereotypes, they are viewed as less competent leaders." However, "Women who adopt a 'masculine' leadership style are viewed more negatively. Although they might be viewed as competent because of their leadership style, they also receive more negative evaluations of their interpersonal skills than women who adopt a 'feminine' style. Hence, even acting in counter-stereotypical ways has potential harmful consequences for women leaders, and may negatively impact their work relationships and access to social networks." Men seeking better work–life integration, a stronger family structure, and a more solid balance sheet at work, would be best served to champion positive, flexible work experiences not only for themselves, but for their coworkers, both male and female, too. Women, although it may feel unfair, should be aware of the double bind and frame their negotiations and requests in terms of how they benefit the organization, rather than just appearing as if they are advocating for themselves.

Likewise, non-breadwinning women, and men, must work together to create a gender-balanced experience outside the office. Diversity is good for all organizations, not just the corporate ones. A study from the National Congress of Parents and Teachers and the National Center for Fathering reported more than half of the men they surveyed attended school parent meetings, a number that had increased significantly in the last ten years. There is opportunity in that trend. As more men take on what have been considered traditional female roles outside the office, it's bound to impact their perspective in the office. Plus, diversity is good for any organization whether it's the company or the PTO.

A Gender-Diverse Ecosystem

When my children started at their new elementary school a few years ago, my husband kept to himself when he took our kids to the school playground, which was mostly filled with mothers. His lack of a social network affected our family. Because he didn't have relationships with the other parents, my children had fewer playdates and we had no backup options for drop-offs and pickups. By the end of the year, however, he had built a solid network of mothers and fathers—a minor issue perhaps in the grand scheme of things, but this kind of progress is the beginning of a gender-diverse ecosystem in which we are raising our children, one that reflects the realities of today's families.

Language is another seemingly small issue that can make a difference in how we view this new ecosystem, too. Here are my reflections on the language we use to describe work and parenting.

The other night I had dinner with a fellow blogger. I asked her if she blogged full time or if she worked too. She replied, "Oh no, I hardly have any time to blog. I'm a full-time mom."

Oh, right, of course. I hadn't even thought about how parenting factored into her time management. At first, I felt a twinge of guilt that I hadn't considered this woman's "most-important" job.

Then I started to think.

I am a mother and I work full time in an office. Plus, I blog. My full-time office job is very important because it feeds my family. My blogging job is important because it feeds my soul. I never think about parenting as a job. It's just a fact. I have a family.

And then I thought some more.

If I am a full-time worker, does that make me a part-time mother? And if I run a small business in addition to my day job, what does that make me? A really crappy mother?

We figured out the mominology for stay-at-home mothers a long time ago. I never ask a mother, "Do you work?" I ask, "Do you work outside the home?" because I know that what women do in the home is work. But if they respond, "No, I am a full-time mom. How about you?" What should I say?

I could say, "Part-time mom here. I was full-time, but I scaled back. I wanted more time to spend with my employer."

Or, "Me? I parent about ten to twenty hours a week. Sometimes more if there's a lot to do. It's nice. It gives me the flexibility to do other things."

Or maybe, "I was parenting but everything was falling apart around me. So I am full-time at the office again. I just couldn't do both."

Or perhaps, "Yes. I work. And between you and me, sometimes I feel like giving birth was a waste because I never use my parenting skills, but I just really didn't want to be home every day so I quit. Maybe I'll go back some-day, after the business is more stable, but right now my clients need me."

I decided to do some math. There are twenty-four hours in a day, less the ten hours my kids sleep. That leaves fourteen hours. Less the six hours they're in school. That leaves eight available hours. And out of those eight, I am gone—commuting or working—for four.

But I am always a mother. I sit in my car during the morning commute worrying about my son's spelling test and my daughter's new friendships. I take a call from the school nurse in the middle of a team meeting. I e-mail their soccer coaches and schedule playdates from my desk.

So I think the next time someone says, "I am a full-time mom. How about you?" I will respond, "Me? I par-ent enough hours to get full benefits."

LESSONS FROM THE LADIES

WOMEN:

- Network outside your own organization and your own industry.
- Welcome fathers into parenting circles and groups at school and in your communities.

EMPLOYERS:

- Close the gender-based wage gap. Offer equal pay for equal work.
- Provide employees with paid sick time.
- Provide adequate parenting leave to support young families.
- Consider child-care benefits for employees.
- Institute flexible hours, reverse commutes, and tele-commuting options.
- Revamp employee assessment tools to remove hidden biases.
- Make networking accessible and welcoming for all employees.

SPOUSES:

- Advocate for parenting benefits rather than moms-only benefits at work.
- Take advantage of leave and flex benefits as appropriate.

6

So, Can We Have It All:
Redefining Success

One night after work, ten women gathered to discuss how they manage family and career. "Don't you think part of the problem is all the literature about having it all?" one of the women asked the group. "Do you think we put a lot of pressure on ourselves that we have to want all that?"

"I think there's a backlash against [the idea that] we have to have it all," said another, an HR director for a large insurance company. "Did you read that article?" she asks the group, referring to the *Atlantic* piece by Anne-Marie Slaughter, in which she discussed the difficulties of balancing her high-powered position at the State Department with her responsibilities to her teenage sons.

Ask ten women about having it all, and you're likely to get ten different answers. Some women feel like the concept of having it all is a bill of goods and can never be attained, painted as a woman's problem, but never a man's. Others use it as a mantra that helps them strive to meet their life dreams. Still others point out that whether or not you can have it all depends on how you define all. "All," one woman wisely tells me, "is whatever you're willing to accept."

Can Men Have It All?

My neighbor the research consultant says, "I think the thing about women can't have it all…I have never met a man who has it all. And so I think the women can't have it all thing is totally a gender-bias assumption." She cites her father as an example. When she was a child he wasn't around much because he was so focused on his career. "I really met my dad in my twenties. I didn't really know him as a kid, and he's now very successful. He's well respected in his field. He was never an academic and now he's working on his PhD. But he has never had it all. So I think, you know, the idea of success as being a CEO at the expense of your relationship with your kids or your parents or your partner, I don't think that's having it all."

"I think the whole 'we can have it all' stuff is utter bullshit," says Kate. She and her spouse both work full time and are raising two children. "You have to decide what's enough. I have no qualms or guilt. It's prioritizing and deciding what's right and deciding it doesn't have to be all. It doesn't have to be Pinterest perfect. We have heat and water. Our priorities are our jobs, our family, and spending time with the kids."

"This idea you can have it all, I don't think you can," says Jen Hancock. "If you want to be rich, something else has to give." Hancock was an executive director of a nonprofit and is now an author who works out of her home. Her husband works in sales, and travels frequently. They have a seven-year-old child.

"Now I'm doing my own thing. I worked my way back up. For me, I want to be home and present—not just home, but present mentally so I can focus on him. In order to do that, I have to be self-employed, and I have to be okay with not accomplishing everything I want to accomplish."

Something Has to Give

Lynn, a mother of two teens, agrees with Jen Hancock's assessment that women need to prioritize and choose what part of the "all" they want. "We're led to believe you can have it all and you really can't," says Lynn. "Something does have to give. There is no clear direction. The woman who runs Yahoo! who's pregnant and saying how she's going to run it…I felt bad for her," she says, referring to Marissa Mayer and her decision to truncate her maternity leave.

Lynn tells me she lives in a modest house down the road from a neighborhood full of mansions. She says sometimes her husband expresses envy when they visit friends in that part of the neighborhood, but she tells him, "You don't get a little bit of it. You have to [sleep with] his wife. You have to live in his home. You have to choose what you want in your life. It's worrying about what it is you want."

I ask a college friend, Holly Bario, if women can have it all. Holly is the president of production at DreamWorks Studios, and, career-wise, one of the most successful women I know. "What I think that is sort of funny…it's so hard to judge it because no one ever wins. Someone is always getting the short shrift. Whenever you try to middle it you feel shitty about work or home." So is it all worth it, I ask her? "I don't know anything else," she says, matter of fact.

I Believe I Can Do Everything

Holly's pragmatism is matched by Kyra's optimism. Kyra is an architect and interior designer with three children, ages eight, eleven, and fourteen. She and her husband own a design firm together and Kyra also owns a running-inspired lifestyle brand. "Women think we can do it all. Every day I wake up with one hundred things on my to-do list and I genuinely think I can get through them all."

"It requires so many people to make that work," says another woman. "A good boss, a good team of people, a good friend system. You can have it all but you can't have it all alone." Right, it takes a village.

Sequencing: A Strategy for All

It's interesting that this idea of needing an entire network of people to achieve your all was popularized by former Secretary of State Hillary Rodham Clinton in her book *It Takes a Village*, because it's Clinton who seems to be inspiring another model for having it all—the concept of sequencing. When I asked women to share their thoughts on whether or not they can have it all, many of them expressed the idea that you can have it all, you just can't have it all at once. And Hillary Clinton is an oft-cited role model for that scenario.

Barb Heffner, who founded a successful public relations firm and now dedicates her time to a nonprofit, believes this concept. "Particularly when you're in your thirties...I was really, really still driven and ambitious...it's hard to believe you will be alive in your fifties or shifting careers. But I think the message that there are different seasons in your life is important. It's a real pity you can't have your kids in your fifties."

Heffner cites Hillary Clinton, another former Secretary of State, Madeleine Albright, and Congresswoman and former Speaker of the House Nancy Pelosi as examples of women who have had multiple careers and are in positions of power well beyond their fifties. "There's a lot of runway in your career now," says Heffner, although she cautions that the length of the runway varies by industry. "I do think the marketing professions are pretty brutal for women. I don't think there's quite the age issue in law and finance."

Barb also notes that motherhood often changes a woman's work rhythm, not necessarily for the worse, but it's something for women to be aware of. "Especially for young moms," she says, "one of the things I think is really tough, especially if you are ambitious, you will not be the same professional as a mom that you were before. I think that's one of those dirty little secrets." I understand what she means. Once, when I was putting in some very long hours in preparation for a big event at work, my boss, the CEO who did not have children, told me he was concerned about me finding some balance. "I have built-in balance every time I walk through my back door," I told him, referring to my children. To be honest, after I had children I missed the ability to work crazy, long hours whenever I wanted to excel at something. But on the flip side, I appreciated the new motivation I had to work effectively and efficiently at the office so that I could get home to my family.

Guys Get to Go Full Throttle

Not every woman I met liked the idea of sequencing or was comfortable with the notion that there may be moments in her career where she won't go full force. "We weren't told about that part," says an IT director. "A few years ago I attended the Simmons Leadership Conference, and a speaker there said you can have it all but you can't have it all at once. That was a huge disappointment for me. What do you mean? She was saying maybe there will be five years when you're having children and you're not going full throttle. And most of the women on the panel had different phases in their careers. But I felt really disappointed. I'm really more relaxed about it now, but at the time it seemed a little unfair. Guys get to go full throttle all the time."

"Getting back in is really hard," cautions another woman. "That's why I switched careers. I had been in marketing. But after my maternity leave my contacts had dried up. It would have been hard to start at the bottom." Off–ramping and on-ramping are very real concerns. For every woman who touts the idea of segmenting her career, another one tells a cautionary tale of how difficult it is to leave work and then return.

The consultant who co-runs her home with her husband says she thinks about this a lot. "I think part of the conversation that I want corporate America to have is not that it's too hard, but that it is okay and actually desirable to want to have a season to stay home with your children, to choose that and to celebrate that." Currently, she says, the consequences can be severe. "The punishment exacted on those who step out for a season is disproportionate. The punishment doesn't match the crime," she says.

Keep Your Foot on the Gas

"There's the stepping off versus decelerating," says Nancy Cremins, a litigator, mother of two, and primary breadwinner. "And I think that is probably an important distinction." It's an excellent distinction. While I am a big believer that the experience women gain as a parent is incredibly valuable to any organization, the current pace of business, the rapid advancements in technology, global shifts in power, and a dynamic workforce mean women must be careful to maintain relevance as they navigate these seasons in their careers.

Ruth Nemzoff knows all about navigating shifts in her career and personal life. Ruth has been married forty-eight years and has four children and seven grandchildren. Currently, she is an author and a speaker at Brandeis University, but she has had many different careers in her lifetime. Her life experiences reflect so many of the things modern women are grappling with: housework, child care, parents' influence, a spouse's career, and institutional gender-based barriers at work.

"Family responsibilities both held me back and in other ways propelled me forward," Ruth says, reflecting on her experiences. "I began as a teacher. My parents encouraged me to have a career that fit in with my family. My father was an educator and believed you need to have a career but also a specialty. I was more fortunate than many women my age whose parents did not encourage them to have a career. My husband

and I went abroad to India with the Peace Corps. When I came back I applied for a master's degree at Harvard and was told that I was an excellent candidate, but since I would soon have children, the admission slot would better go to a man. The women's movement made this practice illegal. Six years later I was accepted at Harvard and earned a doctorate there.

"Perhaps because of this initial rejection I became pregnant. However, I wanted and needed to work outside the home. In those days it was legal to ask about an applicant's reproductive plans. I adopted a private don't ask, don't tell policy. The only job which did not ask if I was pregnant was a state job. The boss was a woman with five children. I was hiding the pregnancy and the boss came up to me and said, 'Ruth, I've had five children. I know you're more than three months pregnant, but if you feel okay I'm fine with your continuation of work.' The second wave of feminism has made it illegal for companies to fire pregnant women just because of their pregnancies. At the time, working while pregnant and showing was not protected. After I had my baby, I began a job share at Goodwill Industries with a woman with high school–age children.

Job Sharing: A Bargain for All

Ruth and her employer were ahead of their time. Job sharing was not yet a common practice, but the arrangement allowed Ruth to manage a new family and a career and allowed Goodwill to retain a committed employee. "Goodwill had a bargain with the two of us," Ruth said. "They had two heads for the price of one and backup coverage. I would work school vacations when my partner needed to be home and I could easily find extra help. We worked beautifully together. Although this happened in 1968, I still read in the newspapers that job sharing is pioneering.

"Subsequently, my husband dragged me to New Hampshire, which I was not pleased about, because I loved my job. We were working with the Boston Council to find work for persons with disabilities. We were working with many private firms. However, I felt I had to follow my husband because that's what was expected in those days."

Superwoman with a Tattered Cape

Ruth found working motherhood challenging. Not only did she have to change jobs to accommodate her husband's career, she faced criticism from people who thought she should be home full time. "Working both outside and inside the home was very difficult," Ruth says, "particularly since friends and family accused me of being a negligent mom. Before long, someone approached me and asked me to run for office. I had never licked a political stamp before but I felt opportunity was knocking. The New Hampshire legislator position was part time, and the salary was low. However, this opportunity allowed me to make a difference and work on issues that I cared about. I was able to get benefits for displaced homemakers, women who had been married for twenty years and had no rights to their husbands' benefits. I helped open adoption records.

"Working part time enabled me to both care for my children and make a contribution, but at the same time it was very hard. I was responsible for making all the arrangements for the child care for the household. I was aware of the privilege I had in being able to hire help. I also have to give credit to my husband for being willing to change expectations and roles. After trying many ways to organize both my work and my children, I realized I had to set aside time just to organize each week and spent every Sunday night setting up the week. It takes time and energy to bring up children and manage a household. I felt like superwoman but with a tattered and torn cape. Sometimes I would feel like I was absolutely spinning from everything I had to do. I think that is true for many women today."

Ruth says she would not have had the courage to run for office without the support of the women's movement. "Consciousness-raising groups validated my ambitions and at the same time gave me the courage to ask my husband to participate in the home-making tasks. By the time my fourth child was born, the women's movement had changed societal attitudes, and men as well as women were encouraging each other to participate in both child care and homemaking. While men and women still do not share equally, the societal support to share is certainly greater than it was in the 1970s."

Because of her parenting duties, Ruth was unable to participate in public office the same way her peers did. She was unable to attend many events outside of legislative meetings so she overcompensated by being informed and prepared. "I read everything, and thus gained the respect of my committee members and other legislators. I learned there are many ways to be effective. I found ways to be efficient with my time."

Being Flexible Is Key

Eventually, Ruth and her husband returned to the Boston area and she left political life. "I found a job working for a peace group." Ruth says working full time with four kids was brutal: "I was on a treadmill. Parenting in America is very difficult. There is no time to relax. If workplaces can be flexible, families benefit. For example, if a boss can be flexible about arrival time, it allows families to help with last-minute homework or sympathize with a child having a difficult morning. I am a big believer that it is better to look at work outcomes than to take attendance.

"In retrospect I feel incredibly lucky, but I also give myself credit for finding ways to combine work and family. We all need help. In the nuclear family there can be no free riders anymore, whether as wage earners or as parents. It is also important to balance the personal arena, the work arena, and the volunteer arena."

In Ruth's story, I find so many important lessons for today's working women. Not only did she learn to adapt to life changes and overcome obstacles, to create opportunities where others may have seen none, and to ask for help when and where she needed it, but she also made a difference, no matter what position she held.

Before I started writing this book, I was rigid in my belief that true power was found in the boardroom of a Fortune 500 or on the Hill in Washington. And certainly it is. We want women, we need women, to break the glass ceiling and get to the highest offices, the highest chambers—that's where you amass the kind of power, wealth, and influence that can make a real impact. But those aren't the only sources of power.

Dr. Anne Perschel, a leadership and organizational psychologist with more than fifteen years' senior management experience at Fortune 50 companies, agrees. "I very much share your position. I want to see women in those roles. That's where you make the big changes." But she says women in corner offices or in Congress cannot be a universal solution. "We've got to be everywhere—big corporations, growth companies that will be big and powerful...."

Enough with the Political Shenanigans

Perschel points out that many women leave the path to power positions, not necessarily in pursuit of a better work–life balance, but because they "don't want to play the game. It's about the political shenanigans." She says, "I think men accept that's the way it is. This probably results from generations of men being in roles where they did, and still do, what they needed to do as providers. They've learned to live with certain conditions, whether they like them or not; it's just the way it is. Women haven't been in it for generations and so we question the rules, the assumptions, and the games that have been played for many generations. We don't like or want to play all the same games, according to all the same rules, based on all the same assumptions. I don't know if that's a wise or unwise strategy for change." Personally, I'm starting to believe it's wise.

I've always felt like a hypocrite promoting the idea women must strive for the top, when I have blown up my own career several times. I have walked away from "good jobs" on several occasions—sometimes to get away from the office "shenanigans" and other times to pursue a brand new career or explore a more flexible lifestyle. For years, I looked at the shifts and turns on my résumé as a weakness, but now I see them as a strength. My varied experiences, and the risks I've taken, allow me to bring so much more to an organization than I might have if I had stayed on a rigid and traditional corporate path. And what these experiences have added to my life outside of the office is even more valuable. That's because my personal definition of having it all isn't just about career success.

But even though I see strengths in my nontraditional résumé, I still need to convince prospective employers to see it that way. So I would urge any woman to take a serious look at the risks and rewards of doing what I did and determine whether the benefits outweigh the risks, which often include reduced earning power and influence. As Nancy Cremins, the litigator, says, "What's going to be right for me and my family isn't going to be right for you and your family."

The women I met while writing this book have taught me that women can run the world from many different places— our homes, our communities, our volunteer assignments, our small businesses. And we are.

Creating a Powerful Life

Mary is one of the women I spoke with who has created a powerful life, on her terms. Mary is a twenty-first-century Ruth, and like Ruth she has found many different ways to be effective.

A nurse who works in acute care in one of the top children's hospitals in the country, Mary also works in a pediatric private practice. "I've always worked full time," she says. "When I went to undergrad I considered going to medical school. I still kind of kick myself for not going to med school, but at the time it felt like what I did was calling. I went back to get my masters and I talk to high school and college kids about career choices. I have three kids, thirteen, eleven, and eight—I have had the choices where for ten years I was having babies and I worked thirteen-hour shifts on weekends. Did I love working weekends? God, no. But I loved what I did, I love what I've done. I had a unique opportunity to shift with each baby. I spent ten years Friday, Saturday, and Sunday at the hospital. It was a great opportunity. I taught at several colleges. With every baby I had flexibility. Now I work. I had to go back even more to carry benefits—my husband has his own company. I want to be home a little more. And I take care of people.

"I love my husband, and he literally had to do everything on the weekends. We ran the PTO together for three years. We've worked on every tax override in our town to raise money for the schools. I do feel I have had this unique opportunity that I publish, I present. I talk at an all-women's high school. Back in the day, nursing was considered a woman's thing. Now, nursing is so powerful, and such strong women and men go into it. I say to girls, you can do whatever you want, if you really think about it. I have one daughter and I'm going to tell her to do whatever the hell she wants."

As satisfied as she is, Mary doesn't make her life out to be perfect. Managing a family of five is challenging. "I've started to say no to things because I cannot do them, and it kills me. It's so funny, as [my kids] have gotten older, I always thought they'd need me less. They're so busy and they're always doing something, but they need you more. I fight with my husband now about…he does so much but there's so much to coordinate a family. When they do different activities, I'm constantly coordinating pickups. You're always foreseeing the weekend. Who's got a game? Who's got what? I come home from being with dying kids all day and I think, please let the bedroom lights be off. I will pull into the driveway and there's my son asking, 'Can you please quiz me?' "

Second in Command: A Power Position

Like Mary, Ilana, the rabbi who doesn't change diapers, has seen her career path and goals shift as her life changes. "Before I had a husband and children, I intended to be rabbi of the biggest synagogue in the world. My priorities shifted. Now I'm number two—an associate rabbi. It's a really good deal. I will probably never be that rabbi.

"I think we need women in leadership positions. But whether we have one to ten women in the biggest positions or lots of women in number two spots, does it matter? What's the influence of lots of women? Maybe in that second seat, power is radiating outward."

Who knows, Ilana still may end up the top rabbi someday. The women I met with in my neighbor's living room have completely bought into the idea that their careers will have several phases and that the best is yet to come. Says the research consultant, "What I think about my career now—I'm almost forty-four, my kids are kind of getting settled in a good place, I feel my career stretching out in front of me. I have all these great options and I do think—I don't know about secretary of state—but I don't know what I can do. I do like the idea of Hillary having been there for Chelsea." She points out that Bill Clinton was at the peak of his political career when the Clintons' daughter, Chelsea, was young, whereas Hillary moved into her most powerful phase after their daughter was grown.

Surgeon General Someday?

"The career can change," says the doctor and mom of two I met at a neighbor's house. At one point she hoped to be surgeon general someday. Today she is part owner in a private practice and works three and a half days a week, a schedule that allows her the time she wants with her family. "I always think about Nancy Pelosi, so I feel like there's a lot of time, but this is not the time. But I think there are certain times... my mom told me once, life is long and you can't do everything at the same time but you can eventually do everything. And I just feel like...I always think when they're teenagers and they don't want to be with me anymore then maybe I will put in more hours or maybe I will change my career."

The doctor says her work and family decisions were shaped by what she witnessed on the job. "I spent a lot of time in hospitals, watching what different women were doing who were further along than me. Nobody was happy. I watched everyone, and they were miserable, and I watched a lot of people having trouble conceiving and babies in NICUs. I thought I was going to wait and then I thought, I can't wait. I need to know what being a mom is like now, before I make the next decision, before I finish my training, because I think it will probably change how I feel about stuff."

Is Happiness the Goal?

The doctor says her decisions about career and family are based more on finding happiness than finding success. "If the goal is to be happy," the doctor says, "that's a different goal [than career achievement]." Her friend, our host, replies, "Well, no, it isn't—that is the goal."

It is indeed. And each woman will define what happiness looks like for her. Some will choose to participate in a smaller arena and some will choose the big arena. And while we know we need both, it would be irresponsible to downplay the importance of the women who go big. "We are the power in our own personal lives and communities and professional lives. We stand up and serve as role models to our children and professional cohorts," says Nancy Cremins the litigator. "Yes, if you think about the Fortune 500, it's only five hundred CEOs. There is only one secretary of state. But we should strive to see women equally represented in those positions."

No One Sits This Out

Nancy believes we must identify the women who are meant for the big arena, and encourage and support them. "There must be truth among peers," she says. "Tell them when they're copping out, 'You should do this. You can do this.' Tell them, 'I know it's hard but I'll help you.' It is a challenge—the personal versus public needs."

And perhaps that's the answer for the other women who feel the same hypocrisy I have felt. We all will, and should, make the decisions that work for our unique circumstances, but that doesn't mean any of us can afford to sit on the sidelines. As Nancy says, "We have an obligation to pump up those people [who pursue the traditional power positions]. How do we support them and provide them with that network of people? How do we hand them up the chain and leverage our own personal networks?"

One night, a group of women in my hometown were discussing local politics. Several women candidates were challenging incumbents in the latest election cycle—our town lacks gender diversity on its governing boards. Several of the women expressed concern about one of the women candidates based on the behavior of her son. And they categorized another female candidate's campaigning as pushy. Male politicians are not judged on their parenting skills. They're judged on their ability to govern. And they are allowed to campaign and fund-raise without judgment—in fact, they're expected to. Women must get behind qualified female candidates and business leaders, as long as they are qualified, and work for gender equity at the top. We must remove from our vocabulary that cop out phrase, "I'd vote for a woman, but, just not this one."

Nancy says, "We all do have to take a vested interest in those things political and corporate." And that is how women can amass the kind of power, wealth, and influence that can make a real impact on our lives and the lives of everyone around us.

I do my best to stay involved in local politics and to volunteer. As a result, people always ask me how I do it all. Here's my answer.

I am a full-time working mother—in fact, I'm the family breadwinner. I am also president of the PTO, chair of a town committee, organizer of an annual event for four hundred attendees, and I moonlight as a freelance writer. "It's easy," I tell them. "But my house is always dirty and I have no friends." And then the person who asked the question always laughs. But I'm not joking.

My house is dirty. While my husband has the time to clean, he has no interest. And I have neither the time nor the interest. Type A personalities like me thrive on checking things off a to-do list, and cleaning never comes off the list; by the time you get through all of the rooms in the house, you need to start over. I don't choose to spend my time cleaning. Nor do I choose to spend my time fighting with my husband, trying to get him to clean.

We used to fight about it. Big, ugly, hairy fights. But fighting wastes precious time, and for a working mother, time is currency. The fighting just didn't add up. Do the math:

Asking husband (three times) to remove unfolded piles of
    laundry from couch and put them away: three minutes
Yelling at husband for not putting laundry away, disre-
    specting all of my wishes, being an insensitive lout,

never listening, and not knowing the meaning of love:
twenty minutes
Giving husband silent treatment: thirty minutes
Apologizing for slightly overreacting: two minutes
Simply pushing piles of laundry to the other end of the
sofa so I have a place to sit down and snuggle with the
kids: priceless.

As far as friends go, I do exaggerate, but just slightly. I
actually have two and a half friends—two of them I've
known for thirty years. I talk to one of them almost every
day during my commute. And I go months without talking to the other one, but our friendship is strong enough to
withstand the long silences. And the half? Well, that repre-
sents all the lovely acquaintances I make through my many
activities. I would befriend them but then they'd expect me
to call, e-mail, and socialize. And I don't have the time.

Sometimes I get overwhelmed, like when I have too
many deadlines, I'm tired, and there are thirty-eight plas-
tic dinosaurs on my living room rug. Just recently, one of
my cousins stopped by on a weekend morning. Over coffee, I unloaded on her that I was exhausted and couldn't
manage everything.

"You need to lower your standards," she said.

As I slid the previous night's dirty dinner plates out of
my way so I had a place to put my coffee mug, I said hopefully, "Really, do you think that's the answer?"

My lifestyle is not for everyone. Like all working mothers, I make sacrifices. I will never go scrapbooking, for
example, or host a book club meeting. Hell, I won't even
be invited to join the book club. But despite my busy
schedule, I always have time to read a book to my child.
Now if only I could find the damn book somewhere in
this mess.

LESSONS FROM THE LADIES

WOMEN:

- Define your own "all."
- Think of your career in sequences. You may be able do it all, over time.
- You can't step out of your career completely. Keep a foot in the door at all times.
- Take time Sunday night to plan your week.
- If you can't be the most available, be the most prepared.
- Make your own power.
- Support and encourage women who are on their way to the top.

EMPLOYERS:

- Consider job sharing as a viable staffing option.
- Don't underestimate the value of flexibility.

7

The Emergence of Entrepreneurship:
Why It Works for Some Women

As women define what having it all means to them, many are choosing entrepreneurship as the path that works for them. According to American Express OPEN's *State of Women-Owned Businesses Report*, there are more than 8.3 million women-owned businesses in the United States, representing approximately $1.3 trillion in revenue and employing almost 7.7 million people. The growth of these businesses has outpaced all but the largest publicly traded companies. The number of women-owned businesses increased 54 percent between 1997 and 2012, a time when the number of total businesses in the United States increased by only 37 percent. And women CEOs aren't just excelling in stereotypical women-friendly industries; in the construction industry, for example, 13 percent of women-owned firms are generating more than $500,000 per year.

Another report, this one from the Guardian Life Small Business Research Institute, projects that much of the country's future job growth will be generated by women-owned small businesses. The report states that by 2018 female business

owners will be responsible for creating more than five million new jobs, more than half of the jobs all small business are
expected to generate.

Are Women-Led Businesses Transformational?

Interestingly, the report predicts the rise in women-owned
businesses will transform the workplace because women business owners "create their own businesses for a variety of reasons, but the most common theme is their dissatisfaction with
the corporate track."

For many women, that is certainly the case. As one entrepreneur said, "Middle corporate America absolutely destroys.
It's full of the Willy Lomans of the world," a reference to the
character from *Death of a Salesman*.

Barb Heffner certainly tried to change the dynamic for
women when she started her firm. "I think a lot of women run
their own businesses to call the shots," says Heffner. Heffner
started the business when her son was six, and by the time he
was twelve she wanted more time at home. She let her business
partners know she was not going to take on any more clients.
"You're going to make a little less salary, if you're not carrying
as much revenue, but there's flexibility. But it is a buck-stops-
here issue. I had an uncle who ran a kitchen cabinet business.
He said, 'Never run your own business.' There are a lot of
tradeoffs. The thing I was able to do, when my son was twelve,
and I'm incredibly grateful to my partners, I started taking
two months off in the summer. They knew if there was some
big thing that came up I'd be there, but for the most part, I
was able to get the time. I did the summer hiatus for my last
seven years at the firm, having varying levels of responsibility from year to year with varying levels of success." Barb says
some summers she spent more time online working than she
had planned.

Barb got to work early and left the office at five. As working from home became more acceptable to clients, she took advantage of the flexibility. And like so many working mothers, she was back online after her son went to bed. "The key to making all of this work is marrying someone really supportive," she adds. "Not everyone is that lucky."

Understanding that point, Barb worked hard to make her firm a place where women could flourish. "As female managers, we have to give women some latitude out of sheer compassion. After my son was in high school and more independent, I tried to make it easier on the women we employed. I'd say to them, 'I mean it, really. What can I do to help you?' You have to persuade that employee that you want to help. I had this wonderful colleague. She had no kids, she was just compassionate, and when my son was sick, she'd say, 'What can I take off your plate? You need to go home.'"

Barb says the women who helped her along the way knew she would do the same for them. "I'd say, 'Go. Call me from the car, tell me what you need to get done.'"

The Camaraderie of the Working Sisterhood

Juli, a divorced mother of two, confirms that Barb created a positive environment; she worked for Barb for many years, including through her divorce. "We separated when my youngest was ten months old. I was in the throes of my first big professional promotion. I knew I really had to make a run at this financially, because I wasn't going to have as much financial support from my husband. Luckily, I had a good support system of family, friends, and neighbors. I knew there was a strong camaraderie of the working mother sisterhood.

"Mentorships are really important too. I was [there] not because I loved the agency work all the time or the clients but because Barb was so great and my colleagues were so supportive—I could race out to a 3:00 p.m. doctor's appointment. When Elliot was born, I was working four tens. I had one day off, usually Fridays.

"I'm really grateful for that. Ten years ago there wasn't quite the same work-from-home flexibility, but I started working Wednesdays from home. It was a huge relief to have one day to not rush in the morning."

Business Ownership As a Path to Flexibility

While some women start companies to build a new culture, others are simply seeking a more manageable work–life fit. Nadia McKay is a mother and former corporate type turned entrepreneur. She is the president of Mom Corps Boston, a professional staffing company that specializes in flexible workplace solutions. Nadia tells me that after she had her first child, she realized the career path she was on was no longer what she wanted. "It's not how I viewed being a mother. I was lucky to have a mentor–sponsor who architected a new role for me. It was a great job that suited my personal strengths. I did it for six years with four different bosses."

Nadia eventually negotiated a four-day-a-week schedule, with one day working from home. "At this point I had two young boys. The job was great on paper but I was still working fifty-five hours a week and getting paid 80 percent."

Then Nadia experienced her perfect storm. "It was the first day of kindergarten. My camera broke. I got a call from work there would be layoffs. At the end of the day my nanny quit. I went from fearing for my job to my husband and I looking at each other and asking, is this what we wanted. I wasn't the mother I wanted to be. I wasn't the worker I wanted to be. I wasn't the wife I wanted to be.

"I took a huge leap of faith—I was the primary breadwinner—and met with a financial planner. We went through a painful exercise but I figured out I could take a couple of years and go back part time, and so I raised my hand for a package."

Nadia's plan was to take at least a year and a half off, but after six months she got a call from a woman and it changed her plan.

"She told me about Mom Corps and it just resonated," Nadia says. "I had to go do it. It was hard because I really wanted to do this but I also wanted to take time off." So Nadia started out working ten hours a week sourcing candidates. "In the end, I bought a franchise and never looked back. It's been phenomenal. I'm working as hard as I ever have but I have the flexibility to do it on my own terms."

She says she works the same number of hours she did at her corporate job but she is able to take her children to school and her mother to appointments. "That one shift in having the flex has made the total difference. I'm doing better financially. I'm there when [the kids] get home from school. I definitely have long days, no doubt about it."

Even as her own boss, Nadia struggles to manage all parts of her life. "Sometimes I get super, super busy and hire a babysitter." She cooks dinner every night and works while her husband cleans up, and she has cut out television and reading.

One of the things Nadia definitely does not miss about corporate America is what I call forced fun, those after-work events designed to build team and culture. For many working mothers, these events are just another obligation, one more thing they need to balance, one more night away from their families. "I'd get dinged on performance reviews for not going to team birthday parties," says Nadia. "I had an infant at home."

Pursuing a Passion As CEO

Work–life balance was not a key motivator for Kyra, who founded two businesses. Passion was. Kyra and her husband co-own an architectural business. "When our children were young we decided that in order to have a more flexible schedule, we would open our own architecture design firm," she tells me. "We were both trained as architects but I leaned more toward interior design, which lends itself to a short attention span. It gave me the time I wanted with my children and allowed me to do something I love. I really enjoy working with people and the gratification of seeing a completed project."

Soon Kyra was looking for a way to get more involved with her community. As an avid runner, she helped organize a road race intended to support a local charity that supports women and girls. A few years into the race she started selling hats and T-shirts emblazoned with the words "Women Run," and realized the idea was too powerful to keep for just one road race. She now designs activewear and lifestyle gear for women who are busy running their lives, and donates a portion of the sales to charities that support women and girls.

"Women Run is growing and so is my interior design business," Kyra says. "I love design; I always felt like I could do more and help more people with my design skills and I am making that a reality."

Kyra is clear that she wants Women Run to inspire others and to make a profit. "I was raised with a very supportive family that instilled in me a great deal of self-esteem. I have daughters and I want them to feel the same self-confidence. Originally the model of the business was going to be nonprofit but I realized it needed to have a double bottom line, helping me as well as helping others. Women tend to lean toward the nonprofit world and volunteer work, which is very important, but more and more women are starting to ask for what they want, for the job they want and deserve and the salary they want and deserve. Women Run is a for-profit that has a nonprofit component—it's purchasing with a purpose."

Managing the new venture, the architectural firm, and her family is a challenge for Kyra. "We used to have a housekeeper, which was fantastic. But I took that money for the new business. I've had to let go. With my first child I thought I was

Martha Stewart. Friday nights I was home cleaning, and that's not what I want to do. I want to socialize. And my kids won't die. And then every once in while I pull a Mommie Dearest moment and scream at everyone."

Like Kyra, Elizabeth, who was raised by very traditional parents, is as focused on her family situation as she is her business. Elizabeth co-owns a branding firm in Manhattan and has fifteen employees. "I've always been more of the aggressive career-focused person," she says. "I'm very lucky that I have a very evolved husband who is very nurturing." The couple has a toddler and her husband has an adult son. "I really wanted to have a child when his son was turning eighteen. When our daughter was born [my husband] was working for a corporate law firm marketing department."

Elizabeth says that, as their daughter started to outgrow the nanny, her husband was becoming disenchanted with work and wanted to freelance, so he quit his full-time gig. "He's a very natural father and caregiver, and I love it because I feel like one of the parents is home. House wise, all I do is laundry. He does a lot of the cooking; he's a better cook. We have someone who cleans every two weeks."

Elizabeth says she and her husband frequently discuss their family arrangement. "I check in and make sure he's happy with it."

Whether women are starting their own companies to make money, find work–life balance and flexibility, or pursue a personal passion, they are inevitably growing the working sisterhood Barb mentioned. And that sisterhood is going to yield more options and new opportunities for even more women.

Where's the Funding for Women?

While we're seeing a significant rise in woman-owned businesses, women still face several obstacles to creating and sustaining their own companies, and managing their family life is only one of them. One of the major challenges is a lack of access to funding. Women make up less than 10 percent of venture capitalists at the top firms, according to a report titled *Gatekeepers of Venture Growth: The Role and Participation of Women in the Venture Capital Industry.* The Diana Project, an organization that raises awareness of women business owners, produced the report. The report also reveals that women entrepreneurs receive just 4 to 9 percent of all venture funds in the United States.

The lack of women in the venture business is part of the problem. People do business with people who look, walk, and talk like them, and so the mostly white, male investors tend to fund white, male entrepreneurs. The gender bias showed up in a very visible way when, in April 2011, angel investor Paige Craig published an article in *Business Insider* titled, "VC CONFESSION: I Have Doubts Once I Think of Women Founders Having Kids and Being Distracted from Work." In the piece he shared a concern he had about a woman who had pitched him for start-up money: "A pregnant founder/CEO is going to fail her company," he wrote. "I'm thinking how in the hell is this founder going to lead a team, build a company and change the world for these businesses carrying a kid around for the next few months and then caring for the kids after. I can't say I personally know anything about it but birthing & raising kids seems like the toughest job around. And now I have a founder who has to be a CEO and a mother."

Craig says he shared his thoughts publicly because he recognized how much talent women represented and wanted to raise awareness of women in the workplace. Jessica Jackley, the entrepreneur in question and cofounder of ProFounder, wrote in a response, "I've never heard someone ask the same of a Founder/CEO/Dad, worrying about a slightly different dirty little thought: 'An expectant father/CEO will fail his company.' The idea that mothers are the de facto 'foundation parents' to a new baby (or two) perpetuates the stereotypes and structures that make it more difficult for anyone, male or female, to balance work and family in the first place."

Ultimately, Craig decided to invest in Jackley and Pro-
Founder.

Lifting the Veil on Female Entrepreneurs

In order to balance the gender gap in funding, we need to balance the gender gap in the venture capital industry. Despite a
business climate that seems stacked against them, women need
to ask for funding more frequently than they may have in the
past. Funders need to recognize inherent biases built into the
process and work to overcome them, and the media should seek
to promote women founders more prominently. We are so much
more likely to hear about Jack Dorsey, founder of Twitter, or
Andrew Mason, founder of Groupon, than we are to hear about
Lisa Stone, Jory Des Jardins, and Elisa Camahort Page, cofound-
ers of BlogHer, or Rashmi Sinha, founder of SlideShare.

We can support the creation of more female entrepreneurs by
encouraging women to pursue careers in the STEM—science,
technology, engineering, and math—industries too. Despite the
fact that women represent almost half of the workforce, they
represent less than 25 percent of STEM workers, according to
the Census Bureau's American Community Survey. Not only
do jobs in these industries tend to have higher than average
salaries, technology and engineering backgrounds are in high
demand in the start-up community. I went to a lecture given by
Sheryl Sandberg, Facebook's chief operating officer and author
of *Lean In: Women, Work and the Will to Lead*, and she shared
advice for parents of daughters. She said to enroll our girls in
tech camp and buy them iPads to encourage their interest in
technology-related careers.

As more women pursue entrepreneurship, their small businesses will yield big changes in the way we think about work
and passion and the way we balance career and family.

LESSONS FROM THE LADIES

WOMEN:

- Build a company that supports other women.
- Examine your finances before you start a new venture.
- Give yourself permission to make a profit.
- Check in frequently with your spouse and family. The business affects them too.
- Consider a career in a STEM field.

EMPLOYERS:

- Don't make after-hours socializing mandatory.
- Level the funding playing field. Women-owned ventures are currently underfunded compared with men's.

8

You Wash, I'll Dry:
Negotiating Tips for Women

A s women get clear about what they want and begin to set their compass in the direction they want to go, they need additional tools to help them navigate their own perfect storm. And one of the most powerful yet underutilized tools is negotiation.

Whether they are looking to change their hours in the office, work from home one day a week, get a raise, strike a deal with a neighbor to change car-pool duties, or get some help with the dishes, women need to negotiate. Many women I spoke with pointed out that when they changed their workload—returned to work after being home with their children, started a new business, or took on a new assignment at work—they failed to renegotiate their responsibilities at home and found themselves in a no-win situation. And fear of negotiation is a contributor to the gender-based wage gap as well. While we cannot discount the biases women face in the workplace as a major contributor to the gap, many bosses report that women don't ask for raises at the same rate men do and that women are more likely than men to accept an offered starting salary without asking for more.

Why Women Don't Negotiate

Women who don't negotiate have a number of reasons why they avoid it.

1. It's uncomfortable and goes against their "good girl" personality.
2. They fear a backlash for appearing too aggressive and pushy.
3. They know how to negotiate at work but not at home.
4. They've never tried it.

Lisa Gates, cofounder of She Negotiates, says women are conflicted about negotiating. She says women have an internal dialogue that sounds like this: "I want my life to look like this but I am afraid to ask for it. Or, I'm afraid I might change my mind about it." To help women get past their doubts, she tries to help them focus on what they want for themselves. "I always drag the conversation down into the personal," says Gates, "because you're going to make a choice from there. I just want women to have access and choice and freedom and the ability to, in the moment, stand up for themselves and what they think and want at that moment."

Carol Frohlinger, coauthor of *Her Place at the Table* and *Nice Girls Just Don't Get It*, says negotiation is a mind-set. "It's about recognizing, welcoming and understanding at a really core, visceral level what you want. If you are willing to negotiate, you *can* change your lot," she says.

Stop Being a Good Girl

Before they can become strong negotiators on their own behalf, women need to get past the idea that they must be "the good girl." So many women create the good girl persona, starting with the good daughter, then the good student, the good

employee, the good wife, the good mother, etc. As lawyer Nancy
Cremins says, "We work really hard and try to put as many gold
stars next to our names from the time we are in kindergarten."
And by casting ourselves in that role over and over, we begin to
believe that's what others expect of us. And perhaps it is.

When women star in the good-girl role at work, they view
their jobs as meeting or beating expectations, making their clients' and bosses' lives easier, and trying to only solve problems—
and never to cause them. That's not a bad way to operate at work,
except if women view asking for a raise as being out of alignment
with their good-girl character.

But if we go back to what Lisa Gates says and truly think
about what we want for ourselves, we might see that asking for
a raise is a good thing to do. For starters, by asking for what
we want, we are giving our bosses a chance to meet our needs.
And in meeting our needs, we are helping the boss retain a
good employee. If you are truly as good as the role you've cast
yourself in, then the boss probably wants to hold on to you. So
asking for what you deserve can only help both parties "negotiate" a satisfactory working relationship.

And there's another reason we should all ask for what we
deserve—there is another good-girl role we could be playing:
good woman. As women, one of the greatest strengths we have is
our network, or sisterhood, of other women. And when we work
together, we are powerful. Being the good woman means using
your good-girl tendencies to support and advance other women.

Negotiate for the Greater Good

What if, during negotiations, you stopped thinking about
yourself and started thinking of all the other women in your
network? What if you reframed the thought process to include
the welfare of others as well as your own? Instead of thinking, "Am I being too assertive?" or, "Who do I think I am to
ask for (fill in the blank)?" you could shift the situation and

frame it around your network of women. Your thought process then becomes, "What do women need to manage a family in this economy?"; "How can I leverage my strengths to advance women?"; "What do women deserve?" Suddenly, it's a whole new conversation, and the stakes are even higher. Try the same exercise with your family in mind (What does my family deserve in exchange for my hours away from home?), and suddenly you're negotiating more like a man.

While it can be empowering to view negotiation as something we can do for the greater good, it's still difficult to discount the fear of backlash. A 2005 study by Hannah Riley Bowles, Linda Babcock, and Lei Lai for the John F. Kennedy School of Government at Harvard University confirmed that women are penalized for initiating negotiations. So what can we do about it?

Frohlinger says we need to be careful about what she calls career-limiting moves. "I'd say that the first thing people have to understand is, although companies have policies that are designed to allow for workplace flexibility, if you are interested in keeping your career on track, you have to know what you want."

She says to consider whether the policies meet your long-term goals as well as your short-term goals. "I believe there is still a stigma attached to taking advantage of these policies but I certainly don't think doing so has to be a death knell to one's career. Many company policies are now broader, and don't focus exclusively on mothers. They may include accommodations for dads as well as for those who may have caregiving responsibilities for elderly relatives. But when you look at the numbers, 95 percent of the workers who take advantage of policies such as these are working mothers. Because of that, the decision to use them requires that you consider carefully how it will be viewed by your organization. Some organizations will consider it a forgivable sin, but a sin nonetheless. If you do decide to take advantage, be sure to think about what you can do to make the implementation easier for your boss and your colleagues. You'll be forgiven much more quickly if you do."

Flextime Requires Flexibility

When women are negotiating, says Carol Frohlinger, they need to remember to think through the benefits to the other party. In other words, if you are negotiating to work more flexibly, understand that success requires flexibility on both sides. "Let's assume you decide that you want to work fewer hours," she says. "You really do need to understand how you can propose to make it work for your particular group. Just saying, 'I'm going to take the three-day-a-week flavor,' without being prepared to be very specific about how you suggest that your work will be covered, probably won't work."

Then there is the issue of women who go part time but end up working full time, at a reduced rate, a common concern among the women I spoke with. "Well, I think you have to manage your time in such a way that it meets your needs overall," says Frohlinger, "and I can tell you from my own experience, when you're a working mother it's not easy to separate your personal life from your professional life."

Another fear women shared with me as I talked with them about trying to make career and home work better together was the idea that in order to negotiate at work, you have to be a perfect employee. "It's always easier to negotiate if you're an incredible talent and can't be replaced," says Frohlinger, "but most of us are not in that situation. So come prepared with all of your information. If you're not feeling strong and organized on a particular day, don't negotiate. Postpone. It's really important to not negotiate without doing the homework."

Do Your Homework

In addition to being prepared with details about your contributions and why your proposal is a good deal for both you and your company, your homework, according to Frohlinger, can include figuring out:

- Who else in your company has tried what it is you want to negotiate
- What kind of obstacles they faced
- What objections they heard

"You know going in that there will be objections," says Frohlinger. To overcome those objections, she says to think through possible tradeoffs and line up allies. "How can you effectively trade the fact you're not in the office one day per week, which meets your need for reduced hours, in exchange for an agreement that you will take up a task that the other person may not want to do? Help your colleagues become your allies by helping them to understand they're not doing you a favor—they are deriving a benefit as well."

Successful negotiation also demands energy and creativity, according to Frohlinger. "Think outside the box. Ask, how can this be done in a way I can stay sane and that is good for the business? People who think they're entitled to workplace flexibility because there's a policy in place or delude themselves into thinking it's the right thing to do or that anyone really cares about their children are naive...you can't make it about you."

When I managed a particularly large team of people, I would ask my employees not to tell me the reasons they needed to leave early, take a day off, or come in late. I did not want to be in the position of deciding that one person's vacation request was more important than another person's dentist appointment or day-care schedule. If we remove the why from the discussion and instead focus on the how—how am I going to make this work for everyone involved?—we can help lessen the stigma around working mothers who feel marginalized when their family life interferes with their companies' office hours.

Negotiation Is a Process, Not an Event

Frohlinger cautions that women need to know that people don't expect them to negotiate, so they should be aware, like the study suggests, that they might get push back. But, she says, " 'No' isn't necessarily the end. To go in and negotiate increased compensation and to think of it as one and done is many times not realistic…in most companies it just doesn't happen that way. Negotiating for compensation or flexibility or any one of a number of things that will make you more satisfied is like tax planning; you've got to do it all year long. You don't wait until December 31 and say, 'I should open an IRA.' "

Men, for their part, can work to be more aware of the danger zone women enter when they negotiate, and adopt win–win attitudes. I can recall at least three instances in which I sat across the desk from different men discussing compensation, and I could sense a twinkle in their eyes, almost as if they viewed the negotiation as a game. I, on the other hand, viewed it as a make-or-break moment. I matched the men's confidence with false bravado and succeeded in two of the three discussions. But who knows how much I might have left on the table. The goal is for more men and women to approach negotiation as a win–win exercise.

Years ago, during a particularly stressful time in my career, I worked with a coach. I was young and had a very demanding boss, and I was having a hard time setting boundaries. I was exhausted and emotional as I told the coach about the challenges I was facing. The coach gave me some useful advice to use when I approached my boss about what I needed. She had me point to the table in the conference room and say, "This is a table." The statement was so neutral, so noncontroversial. It was almost impossible to attach any feeling to an inanimate object and a statement that was so matter of fact. She made me repeat the phrase several times, and then coached me on what I was going to say to my boss with the same lack of emotion and feelings of detachment from what I was saying. To this day, when I find my emotions clouding my conversations, I try to remind myself, "This is a table." If we can stick to the facts, rather than the feelings, our chances of striking a win–win solution increase.

Negotiating with a Spouse

Removing emotion from negotiation is much easier for some women when they are talking to a boss rather than a spouse. One woman tells me how she currently deals with asking her husband to help more around the house: "He asks, 'Can I help?' and then I find out [the kids] were late to practice or the homework is not done and then I go into a tirade, asking him, 'What have you been doing?' I'm like, 'You're not a surgeon. You're not God. What is wrong with you?'" Most likely, she wouldn't be asking her boss those questions. While she might think them, she'd probably maintain some level of professionalism during the discussion.

Frohlinger says part of the challenge with negotiating at home is that our identities as women and mothers are wrapped up in the situation. Then there is the fact that there is no monetary value assigned to caretaker roles. "If you go to work and you see you do an A1 bang-up job, then you feel justified in advocating for a promotion," she says. "It's different at home because I don't think the value criteria is ever quite as clear as it is at work."

And, Frohlinger adds, "[Your negotiation style] is also very connected to your upbringing and the image you have of what a good mother is, and how that factors in to the way you want to raise your children. There are so many types of negotiations involved in our personal lives. There are the obvious negotiations with your significant other—the mundane who is going to do the shopping and all that stuff. There are negotiations with your children—these go on all the time. Then there are the peripheral negotiations, like those with the other parents at the PTO about things such as who'll run the bake sale or chair the book expo. The hardest negotiations of all, though, are the ones you are negotiating with yourself."

And these negotiations, says Frohlinger, are about defining your all. "Negotiating with yourself in this context," she says, "is about what are you willing to give up in terms of the June Cleaver model."

In order to negotiate successfully at home, we need to move past the internal dialogue Lisa Gates referred to and know that what we're asking for today may not be what works for us tomorrow. Second, we need to think about what our partner values. Does your spouse value family time, alone time, or perhaps some time alone with you? Just as we would frame our work negotiations in terms of mutual benefits for both parties, we need to do the same at home. If we want more help making dinner, what will our family gain in return?

Don't Try This at Home

We need to be careful, however, not to resort to coercion or bullying, something I'll admit I've tried at home. I found I could almost always get my husband to say yes if I badgered him long enough. But his yes didn't always hold up. That's because he would tell me yes just to end the conversation, not because he agreed with whatever it was I wanted. But when I learned to truly negotiate, I got better results.

The answer for me was to trust the conversation and commit to wherever it led, instead of being committed to a planned outcome. By asking diagnostic questions, such as "What are your

thoughts about...?"; "Would you be open to...?"; "Are you concerned about...?" I started to hear yesses that stuck. It's hard to
think, "This is a table," when we're thinking, "I can't take this
any more," but the outcome is much better when we do.

You Won't Get It If You Don't Ask

The best way to get to a favorable result in negotiating is, of
course, to start. Many women I spoke with told me they had
never tried to negotiate. That's probably not true, because
every time we ask someone about themselves and take an
interest in other people's needs and interests, we're actually
engaging in part of the negotiation process. But when it comes
to specific situations, like asking for help with laundry or for a
raise, it is true.

I went nineteen years without ever asking for a raise. I didn't
think I needed to. Instead, I just worked very hard and hoped
my boss would notice and reward me. My strategy seemed to
work, until the recession. After the financial market collapsed
in 2008, very few companies were doling out increases unless
an employee made a case for it.

Before entering into a negotiation about salary, women
should find ways to practice negotiation, and one area that
seems to be ripe for negotiating is gaining some personal time.

Negotiating Exercises

Apropos of the life of a working mother, very rarely in the
conversations I had did women talk about finding time for
themselves and interests outside of work and family. But occasionally, one of them would raise the need and desire to find
time to exercise and take care of their health.

During a group discussion one night, Laura asked, "How
many of us make a priority of our kids' health? Like their dentist's appointments every few months."

"I haven't gone in two years. The note is still on my fridge," another woman responded.

Laura injured her back and waited four months to schedule physical therapy. "It's so hard to carve that time out, and so my health and well-being are so far down on the priority list. It's like getting a good night sleep is way down here," she says, gesturing toward the floor.

A third woman said that, after a particularly bad time at work, she's been trying to reprioritize and put her health toward the top of the list. "The last one and a half years have been so stressful and have had such negative medical repercussions that I'm like, you know, in terms of emotionally crying in front of my kids...Unfortunately for me, I hit a point where I was like, 'Okay, all this is bad for the whole picture.' If I can't take care of my self, I can't take care of my kids. And if it means I'm going to get fired I'm willing to take that risk."

At another group gathering, the subject of exercise came up. "Do you feel guilty when you go to the gym?" one woman asked. A friend awed the group when she told them she gets up at 4:45 three mornings per week. "It's the best thing I ever did," she says. But her friend feels guilty for taking time to exercise. "I see a trainer for a half hour every Wednesday, and I feel guilty for taking that time when the kids are awake."

The women who feel guilty about fitting in personal time say their husbands don't seem to suffer the same angst. "I do two things a week. Which is hard. It's 7:00 a.m. and I'm getting ready to go and my kids are like, 'Where are you going?' And my husband wouldn't even sweat it. I was out one night last week and he took the kids to the Y and put them in child care and worked out. They were out an hour past bedtime. He didn't even hesitate. I would have felt guilty that I wasn't spending time with them, that they were out too late."

"Isn't it crazy?" says another. "You work forty to fifty hours, you're trying to go to the gym so you don't feel like a fat ass, be a good mom, a good partner, be with your girlfriends. And you think it would be great if I could go to a movie. You spend a major chunk of time with people who aren't family, and you beat yourself up. You feel bad about yourself if you don't go to the gym."

Not for one woman. She leaves her husband with the kids every night so she can fit in her workout. "I walk out the door at eight. The kids are going to bed and it feels so powerful."

The woman who works out three mornings per week supports that approach. "What are you teaching your kids? It's good modeling." But she says her workouts were threatened when her husband decided to start exercising too. "Then my husband started going to the gym," she says. "So we have to have a full fight about him taking my morning workout time. I was pissed. He goes two days. I go three. But I was like since when are you mister 5:00 a.m. workout? That was my time."

Remove Your Personal Barriers

Regardless of what women are negotiating for, the experts recommend women do what they can to remove some of the barriers that can interfere with the process.

- Try to shed any guilt or shame about your current position. If you want to negotiate successfully, don't waste time thinking about where you should be or what might have been. Good negotiating begins with accepting where you are today and using that as your starting point. So what if you didn't accept that transfer years ago? Who cares if you took three years off from your career after the birth of your child? You are where you are. Now what are you going to do?
- Don't think you are negotiating from a place of weakness; you are not. You have something to offer your negotiating partner. If you have negative, self-doubting thoughts, call a friend or your mother and have them remind you of what you bring to the table.

- Remember, negotiating isn't about besting someone else. It's about building relationships—or what Lisa Gates refers to as "interest-based" negotiating. The people with whom you negotiate aren't your adversaries, they are your partners. And together, you find a way to serve both your interests.
- And keep the end goal in mind. Imagine what kind of mother and employer or business owner you could be if you had the resources and support you needed to thrive. Let that image motivate you to negotiate successfully.

Remember, the best way to get someone to cooperate is to be cooperative. And most women are skilled in that department.

Here are several resources for improving your negotiating skills:

Online Resources

GetRaised (www.getraised.com) is an online service that helps people determine whether they are underpaid and gives them tools to do something about it. On GetRaised, you can compare your salary against the salaries of people in your area with similar qualifications. By asking a series of questions about your short- and long-term goals, GetRaised generates a customized raise request kit in the form of a letter to your boss. The site also takes you through scheduling a meeting and using the letter to discuss compensation.

She Negotiates (www.shenegotiates.com) offers a virtual training program and customized consulting service designed to help women take responsibility for closing their own personal income and leadership gaps.

Books

Her Place at the Table: A Woman's Guide to Negotiating Five Key Challenges to Leadership Success by Deborah M. Kolb, PhD,

Judith Williams, PhD, and Carol Frohlinger, JD, (October 5, 2010) is full of advice for women, from women, about negotiating their careers.

Ask For It: How Women Can Use the Power of Negotiation to Get What They Really Want by Linda Babcock and Sara Laschever (January 27, 2009) talks about how much women lose when they avoid negotiating things like raises and promotions.

Women Don't Ask: The High Cost of Avoiding Negotiation— and Positive Strategies for Change by Linda Babcock and Sara Laschever (February 27, 2007) explores the reasons women don't ask for what they need, want, and deserve at home and at work—and discusses how they can develop the skills to do so.

No Excuses: Nine Ways Women Can Change How We Think About Power by Gloria Feldt (February 28, 2012) encourages women to step into positions of power and leadership.

For Businesses

Negotiating Women, Inc. (www.negotiatingwomen.com) provides training and consulting for organizations that want to recruit, retain, and advance women.

LESSONS FROM THE LADIES

WOMEN:

- Get clear about what you want.
- Don't be a good girl when it comes to negotiation.
- Remember, flexibility at work requires that you be flexible too.
- Do your homework before you start negotiating.
- Ask diagnostic questions.
- Make your own power.

EMPLOYERS:

- Be aware of workplace barriers and gender-based backlash for women who negotiate, and seek to eliminate them.

9

A Cautionary Tale: How Businesses Can Support Women

We can tell women to lower their standards around housework and child rearing. We can give them negotiating tools and training so that they can advocate for more support at home and higher wages at work. But unless and until organizations are willing to take a hard look at how they can embrace working women as a vital and vibrant part of the workforce, we risk losing an incredible talent base, and the brain drain Holli described will continue. And if it continues, we can expect to see the same results we've seen to date. As we've noted, there is an overwhelming body of evidence supporting the fact that women at work, and in leadership roles, yield positive results for families, businesses, the economy, and society. We can ignore that data or we can make some significant shifts in the way we work in order to reap the benefits. But we need to move forward, not backward.

Yahoo!'s Bad Decision

One Friday afternoon in February of 2013, Marissa Mayer, Yahoo!'s CEO, had her Human Resources Department issue a memo revoking all work-from-home arrangements across the organization. The decision was a major setback for work–life advocates who have been touting the benefits of flexible arrangements. It was also a wake-up call that one woman at the top of an organization does not automatically make a company family-friendly. True work–life arrangements are a cultural shift, not a personality-driven move, or even a simple top-down mandate.

"To become the absolute best place to work, communication and collaboration will be important, so we need to be working side by side," Mayer's memo read. Never mind the irony of an Internet company requiring its employees be onsite, the decree was a blow to workers who value a commute-free day, or the ability to drop their children off one day per week, or run an errand without taking paid time off. There's an unwritten expectation in corporate America that today's workers are always connected and responsive to e-mails, texts, and voice mails no matter what time they arrive. "The expectation that people are always available is not helping," an attorney with two children tells me. "[There's an] expectation that you're on your phone checking all evening, the expectation that you'll stay in the office all evening, that constant availability and constant contact." If employers expect that level of accountability, then what can they give in return so that employees can fit their interwoven work and home lives into twenty-four hours?

Flex: The Difference Between Working and Engaging

We can't know for sure whether flexibility made the difference in Juli's career, but we should certainly consider its impact. Juli is the single mother who described her one day of working from home for a public relations firm as a "huge relief" because she didn't have to rush in the morning. Most likely, even without the flexibility and support her boss offered following Juli's divorce, she would have stayed in the workforce; she had to earn a paycheck to support herself and her children. But one has to wonder whether she would have stayed engaged as well. Without the ability to care for her children's emotional, as well as financial, needs, would she have risen to the senior-level position that she loves? The risk isn't simply that women will drop out of the workplace. There is also a risk that they will show up but check out if their needs beyond a paycheck are not met.

Juli would be a CEO today if she thought she could manage that along with caring for her children. "There is a point at which I have to say, 'This is as much as I can do.' I'd love to start my own agency, but I don't think I can."

Still, despite her career success and satisfaction, Juli believes her flexibility affected her earning potential: "You know, I do sometimes think it probably has hindered me financially. I do feel like, even though I was working my ass off, and always met my goals, I'm still working forty to sixty hours per week. I still think that when it came to raise time that because I got a lot of flex, that factored in to my compensation. And I know men doing the same thing as me—making 30 to 40 percent more. I think they think, 'She works from home Fridays and she can't network after work. That's worth $10,000.'"

With more and more women providing the financial security for their families and yet still shouldering most of the responsibility for their family's emotional and social well-being, businesses would be best served to make flexibility part of the culture, not part of the compensation.

"I don't know how a lot of women do it if they don't work for a flexible employer," says one woman. "If their role is like mine, 90 percent falls on them. I'm able to work from home. My manager has said many, many times, 'I don't care if you're doing it at night.' If that's not an option or you have a higher-level job…My husband's former employer was extremely family-friendly. We have a serious medical crisis with our older son, and the new job is *Mad Men*, old-fashioned and not terribly family-friendly. He discussed it during the interview process. He said, 'One of our sons has special needs.' He revealed it during the interview process and they said they were fine with it, and it turns out they're not fine with it. And that part upsets him a great deal, because he's always been involved with it. A lot of it has to do with salary. He thinks, 'I can't rock the boat too much. We'd be in big trouble.' We feel like we do need my salary—but it's secondary."

This woman reveals an excellent reason that flexibility, child care, paid sick leave, and parental leave should not be viewed as women's issues. The flex options for all employees have a trickle-down effect across families. So many women I spoke with depend not only on their own employers to provide flexible options, but also on their spouses' employers so that they can meet the needs of their families without one partner shouldering an unfair and unworkable share.

Embracing Versus Offering Flex

The last time Bess, a marketing executive who works for a health-care company, was interviewing for jobs, flexibility was a top concern for her. And because she did not want to end up like the husband in the aforementioned *Mad Men* scenario, with a promise of flexibility that never panned out, she probed prospective employers very carefully. And the reaction she received surprised her.

"When I was interviewing," Bess says, "I grilled them about, here's what I need, and the senior women were protecting me. They were saying, 'This should be a place that works for women.' It was like this cycle where they almost felt like, and several women at the top said, 'I should have done that when I was interviewing.' It's like they were giving back for what they didn't do.

"I said, 'I will give you what you need from me, but you need to understand I walk out at four.' I didn't want it to be, 'Oh, there's Bess.' I needed it to be part of the culture. And when I started we made a working mom's group and now it's a parents' group. We read through all the perks of *Working Women* magazine. We read through each one and challenged the company to address them. I wanted the flexible feeling, not just the flexible benefits, but the feeling, which is entirely different. Now, if you're remote or working from home, it's entirely normal for people to call in from home. You're not the weird one, 'Oh, we need to figure out a phone.' Now we have meetings to talk about how to be more friendly to remote people."

Brava to Bess. She understood that a company that offers flexibility is not necessarily a culture that embraces it. And when she found one that did, she evolved their attitudes from supporting women to supporting parents. I could have used her guidance and support when my children were younger. Afraid to be identified as a "mom" at work, but needing to work from home when my children were sick (my husband worked outside the house for a few years when our children were young), I would worry during every conference call I made from home that my coworkers and clients would hear a baby crying and think less of me as a professional. Once, when my son was about three, he came into the room where I was working and told me he was going to be sick. I was chairing a call with seventeen participants, including clients from very large and corporate companies like Microsoft, Equifax, and Verizon. I gestured to my son to throw up on the floor and I cleaned him and the rug later, when the call ended.

Can't the Doctor See You on Monday?

Stephanie, the client service associate, whose organization could have benefitted from one of these groups, tells me, "What I get so frustrated about is it's still women having these focus groups. As long as this is a woman's issue, it almost perpetuates the issue." She tells me a story that emphasizes the difference between a company that offers flex and one that embraces it. "When my son was young, my boss said, 'You have Mondays off. Why don't you schedule all your appointments then?' But certain doctors only do Wednesday and Friday appointments."

Bess, when she negotiated her new job, had considerable career clout that allowed her to demand certain accommodations, and she had the skill set to help facilitate them. Requesting flexible work arrangements or raising the issue of fair pay can be risky business for women. Each woman has to weigh her own rewards and risks and determine whether making requests makes sense for her.

Ask Before You Quit

The doctor who owns a private practice wishes more employees would raise the issue of flexibility. "It's been interesting being a boss," she says, "because I've had a few times where I've had nurses who have quit before they've come to us saying, 'This job, my hours, aren't working.' They'll find another job before they say anything, and there are people who are so precious to us. We've told them, 'You're not allowed to leave, so tell me what can we do. We can make this work for you. Tell us what you need. I get it you're a single mom and if you have to work every other weekend and it's the off weekend from your ex getting your kids, you're not seeing your kids.'" The doctor underscores the lost opportunity that takes place when women, conditioned to be "good girls" and not rock the boat, deprive their employers of the chance to retain valuable employees. "We're in a business where we're all about families and we're not going to be discordant about that at all," says the doctor.

Of course, not all industries are conducive to flexible schedules. Jan Risher is a former journalist who left her job to work in corporate communications. "When I was in full-time journalism I was exhausted; the whole ability to control my schedule [is very valuable]...I miss journalism. I really do. It's the irony of my professional life. I had worked my way up. I was managing editor of a cool publication. I loved telling other people's stories. But I couldn't stay. I feel so blessed I have something I enjoy, but the fulfillment from this versus my life...I figured out early on my work did not define me."

In her new position, Jan has found the flexibility she needs to be available to her family. "With the work I'm doing now I have a lot of flexibility. I write, primarily. The owner and CEO gets me and appreciates me. He's okay with me staying up late and coming in late. He totally trusts me to ebb and flow as necessary."

Ladies Only Networking

Sheila, the regional president at a development company, has raised several issues at work—more related to fairness and equity than flexibility—with mixed success. "I don't think women do as good a job asking for their worth as they should," says Sheila, "and I know this firsthand from my situation at work. There was sort of just a huge brouhaha going on with our CEO and my counterpart in another region and another guy, talking about a walkout. I know that, by a fairly large margin, I and the other woman—and we have a male counterpart—are underpaid." Shelia had no interest in participating in a walkout but she did raise the issue of the pay gap with her boss. "And the CEO is like, 'You guys have just got to stop talking about this women versus men thing,' because I've brought it up many times. He's tired of listening to it and I'm like, 'You better not be tired of listening to it because it's real and we know it's real and you have to stop.'"

Sheila had no resolution on her pay, but she was successful addressing an inequity in networking events. "One thing this other woman I work with and I have done is we have a woman's forum. We talk about the guys who are out there golfing, and it's always about guys and their networking and it's just easier for them to do it.

"So we have a forum three days once a year for our clients, and we bring in speakers. At first I thought, 'Aren't we doing the same thing the men are doing?' They've accused us of that; we have to defend it every year. I say, 'I get it. But you're not inviting these women to go and do these same type of events, so we have to.' We make it meaningful and we bring in speakers, and it's a great thing.

"When we first did it, probably four years ago, we had maybe four clients. And at the last one we did there were probably forty of us there. Women love it because they have an opportunity to meet women at all levels. We have women who are younger, just at the start of their careers, connecting with women who are more mature, like myself, and some who are a little bit older than me. It's really good networking."

Establishing multigenerational, women-focused networks is a valuable step businesses can take to support women employees. Still, women need to carefully consider which events they attend in order to use their networking time effectively. Holli has been disappointed by her perceived return on certain types of events in comparison with the time she invested. So, she has become more choosy with her time. She says events for women that are geared toward a more senior level are more attractive to her, as are events that are likely to draw women from different fields that are compatible or related to her own. Events that draw a large population of women who are significantly junior to her, or who are in a transitional phase in their lives, are less likely to be helpful to her professionally. Even though Holli has participated in significant mentoring activities from which she derives great satisfaction, she tries to be intentional about when she is in a mentoring role and when she is networking to build her own career. She says mentoring activities and professional networking are not one and the same, and should not necessarily be done at the same time—although mentors and mentees can certainly become highly valued members of a woman's professional network over the long term.

Finding a way to make board appointments more feasible for women who are already strapped for time and have obligations at home is also an important area for industries and trade associations to tackle. Sheila shared that many of her female colleagues avoid joining boards because these assignments, while critical for building résumés and networks, feel like another job for busy women.

Hope tells me about a board she joined and then quit. "I thought, if I'm going to be on this board, I'm going to go to every single meeting. And they asked me to be on every committee, and I was like yes, yes, yes. And then it was like, 'What the hell am I doing? I need to see my children.' And so I actually quit the board."

Hope says she was attracted to the board because she wanted to do something that connected to her personal passions. "I was looking for the mission piece on top of the work piece. And it's really ironic because, basically, they called me and said, 'You're up for a renewal on the board.' And I said, 'I can't do it. One, the governance sucks and I'm sick of trying to fix this place, so get your act together and call me back. And two, if I'm going to go to meetings they need to be efficient. I'm taking time off work and I'm taking vacation time to do this.' Now, do I get a lot of personal joy out of doing it? Absolutely, but I just said, 'Something's got to give.' You have to pick and choose."

If boards are going to benefit from women's participation, they should consider holding meetings during work hours and they should be prepared to run according to established and published agendas. I have had positive board experiences. I once worked with a nonprofit that was extremely well run. I knew what would be covered in advance of a meeting. I had materials to review. I knew what would be expected of me during and after the meeting. And I could trust the meeting to start and end on time. Those seemingly minor details meant I was able to participate in mission-based work without impacting my work or family.

Google Gets It Right

Organizations can take the lead on offering valuable work–life benefits too. Google, the technology giant, recently did that. Google noticed a high attrition rate among female employees after they had babies—two times the rate for other employees—so the company rolled out twenty weeks of paid maternity leave and seven weeks of paid paternity leave for new parents. Since offering the new benefit, Google has reported attrition has decreased by 50 percent. And Yahoo!, despite its no telecommuting policy, extended its maternity and paternity leave. The company doubled its maternity leave to sixteen weeks and added eight weeks of leave for fathers.

"Would I have stayed working if there was a better maternity leave?" ponders Avital Normal Nathman, the freelance writer, "I do know if we had another child I could see myself going back to a more stable job sooner. And then again, another bonus to having a freelance career, if my child is sick I can be with him."

"Google is a great example," she says. "They saw they were losing women, noticed the attrition rate was not great. They said the point where we're losing was after maternity leave. They decided that was not acceptable and examined how to hold on to women. And they lengthened the maternity leave, extended it to five full months' pay. For an extra two months of pay, they're gaining a whole lot more."

And, post-baby, some progressive companies are catching on to the value of offering child-care benefits. Johnson

& Johnson, for example, has onsite child-care centers so that employees can better blend parenting and work. Employers should not underestimate just how important child care is to working parents—both the peace of mind of knowing your child is well cared for and the ability to place your child in a quality center.

I Should Be June Cleaver

Monika tells me, "As of right now, I'd say I'm earning a paycheck. I've been at my job for a very long time, but because of where I work I get a discount on child care. For me to leave we'd have to make a change, and I'm not able to do that. I do want to work and contribute. I'm extremely career-focused." But she says she doesn't want to "climb the corporate ladder" due to her parenting responsibilities; she has a son with health issues. Monika says, "I feel like there is important work to be done," but she is not entirely passionate about what she is currently doing. She'd like to pursue a different avenue of work. Without child-care benefits, however, she cannot.

"And that makes what's going on at home harder," says Monika. "What's the point? Why don't I just quit? Then I will be able to be the June Cleaver I should be for my family."

Some innovative companies are offering a fairly new corporate perk—one that helps women like Monika be that June Cleaver housekeeper. They are offering housecleaning as a perk to employees.

Housework As a Perk

Evernote, a company that makes productivity tools for the Internet, provides its employees with a free housecleaning twice per month. Interestingly, Evernote executives did not want to be interviewed for this book, because they did not want to position the benefit as a woman-focused perk. An Evernote spokesperson did tell me, "For benefits like housekeeping… it's about eliminating decisions. Having people over? The floor at home has been mopped, don't worry about it. The goal really is to remove some frictions for all employees so they can be more focused and more productive while they're here."

The New York Times wrote about these home-focused benefits in October 2012 and said, "The goal is not just to reduce stress for employees, but for their families, too. If the companies succeed, the thinking goes, they will minimize distractions and sources of tension that can inhibit focus and creativity."

Isn't that just what women have been trying to tell everyone? Take housework out of the equation, and women are suddenly free for so many other high-value, fulfilling assignments.

Who Gets Out at Three?

Businesses are not the only institutions that need to shift in order to support women at work. As so many of the women I spoke with noted, the current American school system is not designed for families with dual breadwinners. Most children are released from school by three o'clock in the afternoon. But many working parents don't get home until after five o'clock. And then working parents must find solutions, usually very expensive solutions, for vacations, nonbank holidays, and the dreaded half days.

Lisa, the nonprofit communications professional, doesn't hold back when it comes to talking about how the school calendar impacts her career. "The school calendar, with twelve weeks off for summer, that's just ridiculous. We can keep it together with camp. My kids don't seem to mind. They have been in year-round stuff since they were infants. You can't tell one general story about working families in America. You could create a class structure based on your child-care options."

Lisa references the inequities in child-care options available to parents based on income levels. Many working mothers tell me summer vacation is a challenge, not only because they need to find programs to occupy their children but because they need to pay for those programs as well.

"How does the workplace even deal with that?" Lisa says. "It's a grind—parenthood in our disconnected, commodified society. The first thing you have to do after you pee on a stick is think about, what am I going to do with this child? It commodifies the kids. How much time am I going to spend? How much time am I going to take off? Time is money. People need to be honest that it sucks."

Where Are the Women in Washington?

Washington, too, must take responsibility and leadership for creating, sponsoring, and passing legislation that supports working families. I always bristle when women tell me, "I'm just not into politics." If you are raising a family, if you visit the doctor, if you work, if you pay taxes, you are political. Or at least you should be.

Working women need advocates in Washington who will champion our causes. A more diverse representation will help. Despite major gains made in the House and Senate in the last election cycle, women still make up just 20 percent of Congress. We need to elect more women at both the national and the local level, and our leaders need to support bills such as the Healthy Families Act, which would set a national paid sick days standard, and the Paycheck Fairness Act, which would strengthen existing laws designed to eliminate the wage gap. At the statewide level, we need to push for legislation that will improve maternity and paternity leave.

If we want to effect change, we need to speak up and vote.

LESSONS FROM THE LADIES:

WOMEN:

• Start a parenting group at work to address flex issues for women and men.
• Build a business case for work–life policies using case studies from other companies.
• Probe prospective employers regarding work–life culture, not just policies.
• Support political candidates who support working families.

EMPLOYERS:

• Rethink how, when, and why you need employees at the office.
• Change the top-down perception that flex is for women. Flex is for everyone.
• Offer paid parental leave.
• Create opportunities "in the middle" for employees who are sequencing and not ready to advance.
• Establish and fund women's networking programs within your organization and industry.
• Make flex part of the culture, not part of the compensation.
• Offer housework as a corporate benefit.

POLITICIANS:

• Support the Healthy Families Act and the Paycheck Fairness Act.
• Advocate for paid parental leave in each state.

10

You're Not Alone:
The Power of Women

Let's be clear. Our spouses, our employers, and our legislators bear responsibility for helping to create an equitable and manageable work–life scenario in the United States, and for eliminating the barriers that have challenged women in the workplace and the world. Our current situation—an inordinate amount of responsibility for housework and child care, subtle and overt barriers in the workplace, and too little representation in Washington—is both unnecessary and unsustainable.

But we are women, and we won't sit back and wait for those around us to change the system. We're going to continue doing more than our fair share. And in the process we can lean on each other and learn from each other.

We Could Talk All Night

While writing this book I hosted several group discussions in living rooms and via conference calls with working women who lead very busy lives. These women couldn't easily get out to socialize on a weeknight, or any night, for that matter. But they were intrigued by the topic and so they made the time.

And once they started talking, they didn't stop. Several of the discussions ran close to midnight, despite the fact that the women had worked all day, and would be up six or seven hours later to make lunches, wake the kids, and rush out the door again—except for Mary, who would be getting up at 4:45 to exercise.

What the late nights demonstrated, for me and for the women who participated in the discussions, is how infrequently we discuss our lives with each other and how much we need to. We talk about our kids. We complain about our bosses, and our husbands too, but we don't really talk about our own lives— what's not working, and what is.

"It's nice to hear other people talk about it," one woman said at the end of the night. "You feel like you're the only one doing it. You think you're the only one getting up, making lunch. You think you're the only one whose kid is in extended day, the only one who can't make the birthday party."

We can get so much from these connections. With a group of women who were all at different places in terms of their careers— two stay-at-home mothers, an elementary school teacher, a business owner, and a nonprofit executive—one woman said, "We need to talk to each other. That's the most important thing. Even if it's just to hear I'm not the only one who thinks I suck as a mother."

It Just Takes a Ten-Minute Call

At another gathering full of well-educated, career-focused women with degrees from Harvard, Yale, and Dartmouth, Hope shared how stressful life was because of workplace politics: "The last year has been one of the hardest years I've had, and part of it has been because my kids have seen me so upset. If I'm going to be with my kids and I'm working all the time, I want it to be quality time. I don't want them to see me crying because I'm unhappy about something and that's sort of my wake-up call. I'm sort of like, okay, you have to take control of the things you have control of and give yourself a break, and I think a lot of women don't give themselves a break."

The answer to the stress, says Hope, is to lean on other women. "You just have to say no to work. It's hard, and it may have repercussions, but you have to recognize you're having other repercussions that are probably longer lasting. I think it's all about trying to find equilibrium. You're like, okay, my pendulum's swung way over here and you have to not kill yourself or feel crappy about yourself. I tell myself, 'Okay, I'm going to do one thing and put it in a box and then make a call.' Call me," she tells the other women, "and we'll talk for ten minutes. That's what I've found is a way to get the pendulum to swing back."

Hope also suggests women form relationships across different age groups. "I think having intergenerational relationships matter as a female. You know, right now I'm trying to figure out the next piece, and I think women who are ten years ahead of me who have made certain choices are great women to talk to. They're not just thinking about the paycheck. They're thinking about things like, do I want my kids to be successful and get a good education and be able to take a vacation? Yeah, I do, but that's not everything. I'm not dying to make a gazillion dollars so they can do all this stuff and I don't know them. To me, that's a failure."

Adulthood Doesn't Look So Good

A group of neighbors, gathered in a suburb of Boston, talked about how their choices as parents affect their ability to pursue their careers. While venting about how weekends are consumed by their children's activities, one woman offered some perspective. "We're not doing a good job selling adulthood to our kids," she said, "if we spend all of our free time going to their games." And in that statement, a few women found permission to carve out some personal time the following Saturday instead of watching a youth soccer or lacrosse practice.

And with a group of female attorneys on the phone one night, we hear a mandate for the feminist movement: to focus on the home, as well as the office. We need to put as much energy and focus behind closing the housework gap as we do the wage gap. Says Jenna, an attorney whose husband also works full time, "I do everything at home. I can't even look at the situation and figure out what will make it better."

Jenna feels like she's already done what she can to make life more manageable. "I have lowered my standards for cleanliness in the house by orders of magnitude. But there reaches a certain level where it's just not acceptable. Or we're eating pizza every night, or we're spending an inordinate amount to outsource.

"It's pretty frustrating and there is a component of it that's sexism. When it comes to being personally inconvenienced, he won't sacrifice his convenience. He's always able to carve out time for himself when he could pitch in on the housework and paying the bills."

Jenna says she's been so stressed out that she's been diagnosed with premature heart fluttering. The doctor's solution? Work out more. "I haven't been able to work out at all," she says. "There isn't the opportunity."

Jenna's friend Grace is hesitant to call the inequity at home sexism. "Not at an individual level," she says. "It's cultural. My husband and I are both attorneys. We both care equally about career. I was able to drop down to four days a week. It was like a Get Out of Jail Free card. It's nice to know I have a day to fall back on. Still, I have to outsource most of it." She says the amount of student debt she and her husband have makes pursuing many other options impossible.

Sydney, another attorney, left private practice for a corporate job. "I felt like a traitor," she says. "I'm supposed to be going for partner. I still want a career that I care about. I just don't know if I want a traditional career."

While these women crave a more manageable life, they wouldn't consider not working. "I like having a job," says Jenna, who some days gets to the office at 2:00 a.m. so she can prepare for her morning cases in court. "I had a three-month maternity leave and I was crawling the wall. I need to be doing something challenging and interesting. That said, I wish I wasn't doing so much of it. But it's not an option to not work full time."

Grace says, "I love working. I need to work. The idea of being an at-home mom would be hard for me. It's about a sense of self." "Opting out is not an option," Sydney concurs. "It's an identity thing."

And finally, Grace lays out a plan for future feminists: "The next movement needs to become more family-focused. Until that becomes more gender neutral...I have the flex to work four days a week. He doesn't have that same flex because of the culture we live in. I do think the feminist conversation should be, how do we fix work, not how do we opt out of work."

"Right," says Jenna. "I would like to work less, not to opt out. But to get more sleep..."

And how much better it is to hear from one another than from the misguided, and sometimes just ridiculous, media narratives about the modern working woman. The headlines are full of warnings for ambitious women. There was the study that reported that men cheat on breadwinners, and that resulted in all kinds of incendiary headlines. But the research, titled "The Effect of Relative Income Disparity on Infidelity for Men and Women," only looked at eighteen- to twenty-eight-year-old married and cohabiting couples. And a new study out of Denmark finds that men who once earned more than their wives but now earn less are more likely to suffer from erectile dysfunction. Maybe men do prefer maids to moguls. But when we hear from women like JJ, Krissa, and Ann McCabe Triana, we know our fears about being breadwinners are unfounded and the hype is just that.

I'm Huge on No

JJ knows how to say no and how to barter. "I'm huge on two things—one is saying no to asks that do not align to my goals and two is outsourcing things that can easily and affordably be done effectively by another person. I have learned that I can be more influential and impactful if I am clear about what I say yes and no to, and essentially where I spend my time each day. There are about twenty-five questions I ask myself before I say yes, such as, 'Am I the right person to do this?' Does it need to happen now? Why am I getting asked to do this? It's about being more aware of what I should say yes to. I always try to connect the asker to someone else if I can't do it.

"When it comes to harmony in my home, it is definitely about teamwork," JJ says about her marriage, children, and child care. "We all support each other's personal and professional initiatives. We could not make it through a week without Microsoft Outlook. We send Outlook invites for just about everything. We have wonderful child care. She is not a live-in but our relationship and her well-being are very important to us and an instrumental piece to my professional success. In fact, she may come early two days a week while the kids are at school to sign them up for swim lessons, get the ski helmet, and do stuff online for me that takes time and energy that I often cannot do until after 10:00 p.m. So she helps with these things and I get more sleep, which makes me a happier mom and employee. We all work together.

"We also have a delightful woman who has been with us for over ten years and comes to our house two days a month. She is our cleaning lady but doesn't always clean. In fact, she is so crafty she sometimes wraps gifts or does errands or even decorates the house for the holidays. When I hire people, I let them know part of the job is house management. What I have come to realize, which was not an easy lesson for me, is that it's not always going to be done the way I want but I've got to let my perfectionist tendencies go if I want to make a difference.

"As I have become more successful, I have built up the team around me. I was there too," she'll tell women who are starting out and struggling. "I worked my way up and before I could hire people to help I would barter my knowledge and skills in exchange for help with errands. For example, I help set up wireless networks or write business plans in exchange for a few errands or a few loads of laundry. Even if you do not have the cash to exchange for a service you can work with neighbors, kids' friends' parents, or family to share chores, pick-ups, or even exchange meals. I have a sister-in-law who helps me in exchange for babysitting time. I've had a couple of babysitters who have been known to do a grocery run for me. I figure I pay them in exchange for time. If you think about it, $10 per hour for a college or high school student is more than they'll make at Macy's, and just think about the time you could gain.

"I have found that my time is my most important asset. So now, I work daily to get most of my commitments—things I have said 'yes' to—working toward activities that will enhance my personal and professional goals. To do this, I need to be aware of what I commit myself to, who I spend my time with, and how I can invest in help when needed. What I have learned is when I give myself permission to focus on the things that matter most to me, I have more moments of joy and fulfillment."

Plan a Sunday Night Meeting

Krissa has successfully created a fifty–fifty parenting arrangement: "[I]t's a really powerful model for running the family and it's a much deeper relationship." She says getting there took work. "This man is an incredibly enlightened man, and it has still taken us two and a half years. One of the tactical practices," she says, "is we have a Sunday night planning meeting where we sit down and review our goals for the year. We review the calendar and the budget. The meeting pops up on both of our calendars Sunday night. Everything falls apart when we don't have it."

Ann McCabe Triana, who has her own financial planning and wealth management company, is a fan of the word no. "I used to be everywhere," she says. "I was out an average of four nights in the week networking, trying to build the business. A good change [since I became a mother] is I am crazy careful with my time."

Motherhood Increased My Revenues

Ann asserts that she's a much more efficient networker and businessperson since becoming a mother. She used to see the potential in every meeting, every event. "Before, I played out all these scenarios in my head. But now, if it's not going to generate an immediate return I don't go. It's the same thing for people who want to have meetings with me. I am just very careful. I am definitely working less hours. Interestingly, the month I came back full time after the baby was born was the highest revenue. And the month after that, we beat it. My partner and I joke. 'You need to have six kids,' he says. You have to say no to make room for better things. I am crystal clear about priorities."

Ann believes being a working mother improves her performance in all areas of her life. "I truly believe I'm a better wife, mother, business owner. It's not just about me any more—that's so motivational and so powerful, and it makes me feel like I'm sacrificing. That's been a really big change. My business has so much more meaning." Before her son was born,

Anne worked sixty to seventy hours a week, including Saturdays, until nine o'clock at night. "It was awful. I can't count the number of times I was going to quit. The good news is, because my husband was a business owner, he was understanding." But the hard work paid off. Anne concentrated on work before becoming a mother and built up her book of business, so that now she is in a position to control her schedule. "I'm in a position where we can control what our culture is like. I would rather be making a little bit less money and have my health."

I Want to Stay Home

We can identify with Ann's desire to have her health and Jennie's desire to be with her children. "I read this article on how women should need to feel ambitious," Jennie says, "and on the flip side, I feel like it's okay for women not to be ambitious. We've made so many strides. We should just be more vocal about our goals."

Both Jennie and her husband work outside the home. Jennie didn't want to put her children in day care, so she stayed home with them. And then her husband lost his job. "The first thirty days, I knew I wasn't going to let him roll with that alone. We're a team." A friend approached her about selling vitamin supplements she was using and she joined the sales team. "It is direct sales but there's a big team base, and they really just help you grow your business. And I also work in my son's school, teaching nutrition one day a week."

Being Authentic

Crystal can teach us about being authentic at work, something many women fear or struggle with. She is an entrepreneur who sold her company and is now working for the acquiring company. She has two children, ages one and three. "I see a lot of women who are creating and building their own companies or opportunities, or are doing freelance and are stepping away from scenarios where they have to be in cowboy cultures," she says. "And it's not really a matter of women lacking the confidence. I don't see that as the issue. It's more about, 'Gosh, my time is really precious. Why would I want to build something in an environment that isn't tied to my own optimal growth and development?' For anyone to work effectively, they have to be in an environment where they can be themselves.

"You're going to be successful if you're who you are," she says. "If the caring and maternal part of you has a huge value in the workplace and you try to hide or stifle it, it's not going to shine. I think people gravitate to want to work and be part of who they fully are. If you're in the C-suite or on the executive team, you clearly have greater power.

"And I think about that for myself," she says. "I feel a great responsibility toward the other women, and, frankly, the other women with families. I know I'll get amazing and incredible work from them."

It's About Forgiveness

Whether we identify with the woman who is a business owner, the stay-at-home mother, the co-parent, or the entrepreneur, Nancy Cremins, the lawyer, says it all comes down to flex and forgiveness. "You have to forgive yourself for not being perfect all the time. You have to forgive you're in an imperfect system. You can rail against it but it's the world you live in. You have to forgive your spouse. You have to forgive your parents for how you were raised and try to move past it."

She says women also have to forgive themselves. "On a daily basis, I deride myself for all the things I'm not doing right—like, I need to get to the gym. You hold on to it and address it and then forgive. You always feel like a fraud; nothing is quite good enough. I'm learning to let go of that."

The Truth About Working Women

We have to forgive each other our choices. The truths about working women are as diverse as the number of working women in the United States. There are women in corner offices and women who plan to enter the corner office. There are women who may not want the number-one spot but are still interested in a high-powered and fulfilling career, regardless of the obstacles they may encounter. And there are women who are happy with a middling career, or no career at all.

When faced with gender-based biases at work; corporate cultures and missions that don't connect with their own value systems and passions; the responsibilities of managing a household and a family; the joy, for many, of being a parent; and any other obligations life presents, many women have said, if something has got to give, I'm fine for it to be my career. When I started this book, I didn't want to report that women were happy to walk away from work—and, again, not all of them are. But a significant number of women I met had a take it or leave it, or maybe just a leave it, attitude, and that's significant.

- That's significant for our economy, which depends on women to grow.
- That's significant for companies that stand to lose out on an incredible talent pool.
- That's significant for women who may not see an alternative way forward, and could put themselves at financial risk by not earning a paycheck.
- That's significant for our children, who look to us as role models and will drive the future economy.

So, perhaps most importantly, we have to fight for each other. We need to work together to remove the barriers we face—at home and at work—and to pave the way for the women who will lead.

As one woman said to me, "Let's get rid of the fantasy that life is easy. Life is tough, you know. You are not required to complete the job, but you must begin. I believe the job to be completed is to change the world of work to accommodate families."

LESSONS FROM THE LADIES
· ·

WOMEN:

- Talk to other women. Create informal networks and meet quarterly.
- Take time for a ten-minute call to a friend when work is overwhelming.
- Be clear about your nonnegotiable priorities. Say no to everything else.
- Use technology to coordinate schedules and chores with your spouse.
- Hold a weekly family planning meeting.
- Be yourself at work.
- Forgive yourself for not being perfect.

ENDNOTES

Introduction

1. "Fast Facts: Degrees Conferred by Sex and Race," National Center for Education Statistics, U.S. Department of Education 2012, http://nces.ed.gov/fastfacts/display.asp?id=72, accessed June 2013.
2. "Degrees Conferred by Degree-Granting Institutions," National Center for Education Statistics, U.S. Department of Education, accessed June 2013, http://nces.ed.gov/programs/digest/d12/tables/dt12_310.asp.
3. Kim Parker and Wendy Wang, "Modern Parenthood: Roles of Moms and Dads Converge as They Balance Work and Family," Pew Research, March 14, 2013, http://www.pewsocialtrends.org/2013/03/14/modern-parenthood-roles-of-moms-and-dads-converge-as-they-balance-work-and-family/.
4. Kim Parker and Wendy Wang, "Modern Parenthood: Roles of Moms and Dads Converge as They Balance Work and Family," Pew Research, March 14, 2013, http://www.pewsocialtrends.org/2013/03/14/modern-parenthood-roles-of-moms-and-dads-converge-as-they-balance-work-and-family/.
   borforce/ "http://www.dol.gov/_sec/media/reports/femalelaborforce/.
5. "American Time Use Survey Summary." Bureau of Labor Statistics. Accessed June 22, 2012. http://www.bls.gov/news.release/atus.nr0.htm.
6. "American Time Use Survey Summary." Bureau of Labor Statistics. Accessed June 22, 2012. http://www.bls.gov/news.release/atus.nr0.htm.

Chapter 1

1. "Employment Characteristics of Families Summary," Bureau of Labor Statistics, April 26, 2013, http://www.bls.gov/news.release/famee.nr0.htm.
2. "Wives Who Earn More Than Their Husbands, 1987–2011," Bureau of Labor Statistics, accessed May 2013, http://www.bls.gov/cps/wives_earn_more.htm.

3. "Share of Married-Couple Families with an Employed Mother at Its Lowest, 1994–2010," Bureau of Labor Statistics, May 6, 2011, http://www.bls.gov/opub/ted/2011/ted_20110506.htm.

4. "Child Care," Family Friendly Work, accessed May 2013, http://www.familyfriendlywork.org/child-care.html.

5. "Fact Sheet: Selected Caregiver Statistics," The National Alliance for Caregiving and AARP (2009), Caregiving in the U.S. National Alliance for Caregiving, last updated November 2012, http://www.caregiver.org/caregiver/jsp/content_node.jsp?nodeid=439.

6. "Women and Paid Sick Days: Crucial for Family Well-Being," Institute for Women's Policy Research, February 2007.

7. "Women and Paid Sick Days: Crucial for Family Well-Being," Institute for Women's Policy Research, February 2007.

REFERENCES

Bureau of Labor Statistics. "American Time Use Survey Summary."
June 22, 2012. http://www.bls.gov/news.release/atus.nr0.htm.

Bureau of Labor Statistics. "Employment Characteristics of Families Summary." April 26, 2013. http://www.bls.gov/news.release/famee.nr0.htm.

Bureau of Labor Statistics. "Labor Force Projections to 2020: A More Slowly Growing Workforce." January 2012. Accessed May 2013. http://www.bls.gov/opub/mlr/2012/01/art3full.pdf.

Bureau of Labor Statistics. "Share of Married-Couple Families with an Employed Mother at Its Lowest, 1994–2010." May 6, 2011. http://www.bls.gov/opub/ted/2011/ted_20110506.htm.

Bureau of Labor Statistics. "Wives Who Earn More Than Their Husbands, 1987–2011." Accessed June 2013. http://www.bls.gov/cps/wives_earn_more.htm.

Department of Labor. "Women's Employment During the Recovery." Accessed May 2013. http://www.dol.gov/_sec/media/reports/femalelaborforce/.

Family Friendly Work. "Child Care." Accessed May 2013. http://www.familyfriendlywork.org/child-care.html.

Moms Rising. "S: Sick Days, Paid." Accessed May 2013. http://www.momsrising.org/issues_and_resources/paid-sick-days-all.

National Center for Education Statistics, U.S. Department of Education. "Fast Facts: Degrees Conferred by Sex and Race." Accessed June 2013. http://nces.ed.gov/fastfacts/display.asp?id=72.

National Center for Education Statistics, U.S. Department of Education. "Degrees Conferred by Degree-Granting Institutions." Accessed June 2013. http://nces.ed.gov/programs/digest/d12/tables /dt12_310.asp.

National Center for Family and Marriage Research (NCFMR) at Bowling Green State University. "More Wives Becoming Primary Breadwinners, BGSU Researchers Find." March 11, 2013. http:// www.bgsu.edu/offices/mc/news/2013/news128738.html.

Parker, Kim, and Wendy Wang. "Modern Parenthood: Roles of Moms and Dads Converge as They Balance Work and Family." Pew Research. March 14, 2013. http://www.pewsocialtrends.org /2013/03/14/modern-parenthood-roles-of-moms-and-dads-converge-as-they-balance-work-and-family/.

"Working Moms Reject One-Size-Fits-All Answer." *USA Today*, March 4, 2013. http://www.usatoday.com/story/opinion/2013/03 /04/working-moms-child-care/1963333/.